Portrait of a Princess

The Truth About You From The King's Point of View

S. Kristi Douglas

PORTRAIT OF A PRINCESS: THE TRUTH ABOUT YOU FROM THE KING'S POINT OF VIEW
Copyright © 2018 by S. Kristi Douglas
ISBN 978-0-692-77047-4

Illustrations by Xenia Rassolova. Used with permission of the artist.

The Royal Decree adapted with permission from Barry Adams, © 1999.

Could it Be? © 2011 S. Kristi Douglas
The Color of Kings © 2011 S. Kristi Douglas
In His Eyes © 2011 S. Kristi Douglas
Forgive Me © 2012 S. Kristi Douglas
Daughter of the King © 2009 S. Kristi Douglas
This Battle © 2014 S. Kristi Douglas
Highest Praise © 2013 S. Kristi Douglas
My Soul's Praise © 2010 Sam Harrell, Nikita Gay, S. Kristi Douglas
Satisfy My Soul © 2011 S. Kristi Douglas
I Can Do All Things © 2013 S. Kristi Douglas

Designed & Published by King's Daughter Publishing
Indian Trail, North Carolina 28079
www.KingsDaughterPublishing.com

All rights reserved. No part of this book may be used or reproduced by any means, graphic, electronic, or mechanical, including photocopying, recording, taping or by any information storage retrieval system without the written permission of the author except in the case of brief quotations embodied in critical articles and reviews.

Printed in the United States of America.

Scripture quotations marked AMP are taken from the Amplified® Bible, Copyright © 1954, 1958, 1962, 1964, 1965, 1987 by The Lockman Foundation. Used by permission. (www.Lockman.org). Scripture quotations marked ESV are from the ESV® Bible (The Holy Bible, English Standard Version®), copyright © 2001 by Crossway, a publishing ministry of Good News Publishers. Used by permission. All rights reserved. Scripture quotations marked HCSB®, are taken from the Holman Christian Standard Bible®, Copyright © 1999, 2000, 2002, 2003, 2009 by Holman Bible Publishers. Used by permission. HCSB® is a federally registered trademark of Holman Bible Publishers. Scripture quotations marked ISV are taken from the Holy Bible: International Standard Version®. Copyright © 1996-forever by The ISV Foundation. All rights reserved internationally. Used by permission. Scripture quotations marked KJV are from The Authorized (King James) Version. Rights in the Authorized Version in the United Kingdom are vested in the Crown. Reproduced by permission of the Crown's patentee, Cambridge University Press. Scripture quotations marked MSG are taken from The Message. Copyright © 1993, 1994, 1995, 1996, 2000, 2001, 2002. Used by permission of NavPress Publishing Group. Scripture quotations marked NASB are taken from the New American Standard Bible®, Copyright © 1960, 1962, 1963, 1968, 1971, 1972, 1973, 1975, 1977, 1995 by The Lockman Foundation Used by permission. (www.Lockman.org). Scripture quotations marked NIV are taken from the Holy Bible, New International Version®, NIV®. Copyright © 1973, 1978, 1984, 2011 by Biblica, Inc.™ Used by permission of Zondervan. All rights reserved worldwide. (www.Zondervan.com). The NIV and New International Version are trademarks registered in the United States Patent and Trademark Office by Biblica, Inc.™ Scripture quotations marked NKJV are taken from the New King James Version®. Copyright © 1982 by Thomas Nelson. Used by permission. All rights reserved. Scripture quotations marked NLT are taken from the Holy Bible, New Living Translation, copyright ©1996, 2004, 2007, 2013, 2015 by Tyndale House Foundation. Used by permission of Tyndale House Publishers, Inc., Carol Stream, Illinois 60188. All rights reserved.

Acknowledgements

For your prayers, encouragement, inspiration, and unwavering support and belief in my vision and gifts, I would like to thank the following:

My mother & prayer warrior, Geraldine Donaldson
My dear husband, Malcolm
My loves, Remington, Dakota and Tennyson
My big brother, Johann Pierre King
Mrs. Dawn Anthony
Dr. Kenya Ayers
Mr. Jim Bethea
Pastor Haman Cross, Jr.
Mrs. DeShannon Dixon
The Douglas Family
Mr. Darek Dowgielewicz
Dr. Vanessa Figgers
Mrs. Mildred Green
Mr. Samuel Harrell
The Johnson-Hester Family
The King Family
Mrs. Sonya Matthews
Pastor Richard and Mrs. Dorothy McMillan
Dr. Vernease Herron Miller
Ms. Tobi Morris
Rev. Dr. Barbara L. Peacock
Ms. Xenia Rassolova, Artist Extraordinaire
Mr. & Mrs. Charles R. Snow, Sr.
Ms. Deneen Snow
Mrs. Mamie Williams

Ms. Cat Winslow
Mrs. Betty Woods
The Courageous Women of Dove's Nest

"I do not cease to give thanks for you..."
—Ephesians 1:16a (AMP)

Dedication

This book is dedicated to my Heavenly Father — my Abba — for teaching me what it means to live as a Princess, a daughter of the King of Kings, every day. Thank You for giving me the courage and wisdom to lead more of Your daughters to this spiritual treasure.

I also dedicated this book to my Daddy, Malvin James King, Jr., who made me a literal "daughter of a King." Until we meet again, may you rest in heaven.

Your Loving Daughter,

J. Kristi Douglas

"The Spirit of the Sovereign Lord is on me, because the Lord has anointed me to proclaim good news to the poor. He has sent me to bind up the brokenhearted, to proclaim freedom for the captives and release from darkness for the prisoners." —Isaiah 61:1

Table of Contents

How to Use this Book   10

Foreword   12

Introduction   18

Chapter One | Who Do You Think You Are?   27
Lyrical Love Letter: Could it Be?

Chapter Two | A King's Ransom   36
Lyrical Love Letter: The Color of Kings

Chapter Three | The Purpose of a Princess   50
Lyrical Love Letter: In His Eyes

Chapter Four | The Preparation of a Princess   62

Chapter Five | The Purification of a Princess   80
Lyrical Love Letter: Forgive Me

Chapter Six | The Promises of a Princess   97
Lyrical Love Letter: Daughter of the King

Chapter Seven | The Power of a Princess   107
Lyrical Love Letter: This Battle

Chapter Eight | The Prayers of a Princess   120
Lyrical Love Letter: Highest Praise

Chapter Nine | The Praises of a Princess   131
   Lyrical Love Letter: My Soul's Praise

Chapter Ten | The Passions of a Princess   142
   Lyrical Love Letter: Satisfy My Soul

Chapter Eleven | The Possibilities of a Princess   154
   Lyrical Love Letter: I Can Do All Things

Appendix   164
   The Royal Decree   167
   Royal Retreat Study Guide   174
   About the Author   229

How to Use This Book

Each chapter of this book explores a new aspect of the relationship between the King and His daughters. Together, we will discover the Purpose, Preparation, Purification, Promises, Power, Prayers, Praises, Passions, Possibilities of a Princess and so much more!

At the end of the chapters in **Portrait of a Princess: The Truth About You from the King's Point of View**, you will find the following:

💎 ***Priceless Pearl:*** A scripture that you should commit to memory. Ask God to help you memorize these verses, which will begin to transform your way of thinking.

💎 ***Princess Proclamation:*** An affirmation, meditation or a prayer that was written to reinforce the ideas and concepts introduced in the corresponding chapter. They provide a practical way for you to actively become involved with your own spiritual and mental transformation through oral affirmation.

💎 ***Lyrical Love Letter:*** Lyrics to songs specifically written to enhance the concepts and ideas introduced in the chapter. You'll find the recorded version of the songs on the MP3 download, *"Daughter of the King"*. During your personal time of daily meditation and praise (and anytime throughout your day), relax, listen, and allow the Holy Spirit to minister to your soul through these original compositions, which were inspired by the Holy Spirit especially for you.

In addition, the **Appendix** contains:

💎 ***Royal Retreat Study Guide:*** Designed for further study (individually and/or with a small group), the *"Royal Retreat Study Guide"* is full of additional scriptures, questions and exercises designed to help you think deeply (and personally) about the concepts introduced and explained in the preceding chapters. The work is challenging, but you will reap tremendous benefit from the required honesty, transparency, candor and discussion, which leads to personal transformation. *"Behold, you desire truth in the inward parts: and in the hidden part you shall make me to know wisdom."* (Psalm 51:6, AKJV)

💎 ***Royal Decree:*** A one-stop shopping list of many of God's promises to His daughters. Refer to this list whenever you need affirmation, confirmation, or validation about your worth or God's desire and power to act on your behalf.

💎 ***Daughter of the King:*** An MP3 download featuring original music written and recorded by **Portrait of a Princess** author, S. Kristi Douglas.

Foreword

I had *finally* finished writing this book.

After eight long years of testing ideas, of writing in fits and starts, I was done.

I brushed off my hands and sent the book to my editors for review.

"This is wonderful," said Tobi, a gifted writer, editor and book designer (who also happens to be a longtime friend).

I smiled and thanked her.

"Except for one thing," she said. I was concerned by the change in her tone of voice. "You never told your story," she said.

"What do you mean?" I asked.

"I know your story, and it's missing from the book. Why didn't you tell it?" she asked.

Her question made me uncomfortable. I tried explaining that it was an intentional omission. Since the book is not intended to be autobiographical, I wanted readers to focus solely on its principles.

"But your story is too powerful not to tell," she said. "Without it, the book feels a bit preachy," she continued. "Although what you've written is true and is very good, if I didn't know you already, why should I listen to you? Your personal story validates your work."

I knew exactly what she meant. But doing what she asked would be much harder than it seemed.

You see, my story is woven together in places by a common "black thread" of sorts, connecting many of my life's events. This thread was the source of my own struggle with shame and low self-esteem.

My first memory of the black thread begins in childhood. Even at a tender age, the enemy was strategic and expert in weaving it through early exposure to unhealthy, inappropriate relationships.

As a young woman, I never felt like I was "enough." I couldn't believe that anyone could be genuinely interested in me as a person. I manipulated relationships in a flawed attempt to experience intimacy, build self-esteem, and exercise control and power. And in turn, I found myself being manipulated in ways (that I permitted) without ever having the requirement of loyalty, commitment or love. This led to a devastating cycle of more heartache and rejection and only served to deepen my distorted sense of self.

I could sense the Holy Spirit prodding me to allow Him to heal my deeply wounded spirit. God wanted to address the deep feelings of guilt, rejection, loneliness and brokenness I had experienced. As I submitted to the process, I finally began to see the light. I wanted to love God and others with the freedom I was starting to experience in Christ. I began to grow spiritually and gained a passion for teaching the word of God to women. I knew what the love and power of God could do. Like the biblical woman at the well, I felt compelled to invite women to "come and see a Man" whose love could quench a thirsty soul like no other man's could.

Although change had begun, another black thread was being woven in an attempt to thwart the transforming work God was doing in my life. There was a time when it seemed that nearly every aspect of my life was beginning to come apart at the seams. I was powerless to change anything and found myself in a very low place.

And that's exactly where God wanted me.

One day, I cried out to God in desperation. I heard Him speak clearly, "If you only understood who I am, you would view this experience from my perspective."

Then He posed a simple question, "Who am I?"

Now, God is many things. There are many different names for God—too many to list. This is why He said to Moses, "I AM that I AM." God is who we need Him to be at any given moment in time.

On that day, I happened to answer, "You are the King."

"That's correct," God said. "And since I am the King and you are my daughter, who are you?"

"A princess," I replied.

A princess?

Wow. I had to let that one sink in.

I certainly didn't *feel* like a princess. A princess is no ordinary woman. I began to imagine the special privileges that come along with being a princess. Royalty. Inheritance. Stature. Authority. Beauty. Wealth...

God sent me on a mission to discover what He meant when He gave me such a special title. In the process, a song of praise and affirmation began to stir in my spirit:

I am a princess, a Daughter of the King.
Let me tell you all about the day it came to be.
One day I heard that the King was issuing a royal decree.
It said that anyone who would receive His Son
Could be a part of His royal family.
Now I'm a princess, a Daughter of the King.

I am a princess, a Daughter of the King.
But this is not a fairy tale. It's real as real can be.
He clothed me in purple, gave me a crown of life
And made me royalty.
That's why I bow my knees. And why I lift my hands.

Foreword

I give Him praise for all He's done for me.
For I'm a princess, a Daughter of the King.

The song was powerful. I could tell its impact when I sang it before crowds of women to whom I was privileged to minister. They often told me, through tears, of the meaning it held for them. Our stories were different, but the message rang clear. I promised the Lord that if He would give me the opportunity and the platform, I would share this powerful message of deliverance to women who need to be reminded of who they are (and whose they are) in Christ.

I was on a mission. I began to chronicle my journey to discover my true spiritual identity. I started teaching in local women's shelters. Inspired, I wrote and staged a theatrical production called "Daughter of the King: The Musical" (www.DOKTheMusical.com). And I began writing this book, **Portrait of a Princess: The Truth About You from the King's Point of View**. In 2015, I founded She Reigns Ministries (www.SheReigns.org), a nonprofit organization whose mission is to "create a world where every woman knows her worth." We offer a powerful, faith-based self-esteem curriculum for women and girls, using the creative arts as a vehicle for the message.

I heard the King saying, "Princess, tell your story. Many more of my daughters need to hear what you have to say."

Looking back, the black threads of my life have been difficult. I have felt the needle-sharp pain of every stitch. But the threads serve an important purpose.

Upon closer inspection, I can see that the threads are not actually black, but rather they are a deep brownish red—the color of dried blood. The blood of Jesus Christ, which He freely shed for all, has covered me throughout this journey. The blood-stained threads connect to form the tapestry of my life's story. Without them, there is no definition and no distinction of my story from any other. They serve to outline God's specific purpose for me in the grand scheme of humanity, which is under His direction and control.

When I view this tapestry from underneath, it looks like a jumbled mess. There are dead ends and knots and tangled places that simply seem to be going nowhere. But when I view it from the high perspective of the One who is weaving *"all things together for the good of those who love Him and are called according to His purpose" (Romans 8:28)*, I can see that He is entwining one circumstance with another to create a beautiful and priceless—yet unfinished—work of art.

Dear Princess, our experiences may be different. There are many circumstances that can cause women to question their worth. Unfortunately, low self-esteem is not limited to young girls. Many grown women still suffer in silence. We put on a good face, appearing as if we have it all together, yet we continue to make poor decisions that negatively impact our futures. We sometimes speak unkindly to and about ourselves. We may live under a constant cloud of unworthiness. Or we attempt to cover our low self-image through our achievements, our appearance, an artificial and inflated sense of importance, and by belittling others.

No matter what has brought you to the point where you sense a need for change, I'm glad you're here. But in order for you to experience this revolution, you will need to be totally honest and transparent with God in the process. *"Behold, You desire truth in the innermost being, and in the hidden part You will make me know wisdom." (Psalm 51:6, NASB)*

I'm asking God to help you reclaim a healthy (godly) self-image. After all, you were made in His image! Once you begin to understand how God sees you, it will totally reshape the way you see yourself, relate to and love others, and make decisions for your future. Even if your physical circumstances never change, you can. I know. That's exactly what happened to me.

My prayer is that through **Portrait of a Princess: The Truth About You from the King's Point of View,** the tapestry of my experience will somehow be displayed for your transformation, your encouragement, but most of all, for God's glory.

"In Him we were also chosen, having been predestined according to the plan of Him who works out everything in conformity with the purpose of His will, in order that we, who were the first to put our hope in Christ, might be for the praise of His glory." (Ephesians 1:11-12, NIV)

~ *S. Kristi Douglas*

Introduction

"For as [she] thinks in [her] heart so is [she]."
—Proverbs 23:7a, NKJV

"We break down every thought and proud thing that puts itself up against the wisdom of God. We take hold of every thought and make it obey Christ."
—2 Corinthians 10:5, NLT

Give me your lunch money!

This scene plays out five days a week on school playgrounds across the country. You've probably seen it before, either on TV or in person.

There he is—the short, skinny kid with the oversized glasses sliding down his nose.

He hovers awkwardly near the basketball courts. He's hoping today the fellas will finally invite him to come and shoot some hoops.

Cue the school yard bully: overgrown, ugly and smelling like old gym socks. He boldly saunters over, snarling, "Give me your lunch money!"

Knobby knees knocking in his neatly pressed khaki shorts, Awkward Kid looks around and feigns deafness, desperately hoping the teacher across the yard will quickly intervene before this miscarriage of justice occurs. But she's too busy gabbing with the assistant principal to notice.

"You heard me, punk! I said GIVE. ME. YOUR. LUNCH. MONEY!" the bully taunts, now chest-to-face with his prey.

Awkward Kid sighs. He's weary of this episode. Week after week he gives up his allowance—hard earned from cutting Old Man Simpson's grass—to a bully who can barely even count it. As he reluctantly reaches into his pocket, fondling the neatly folded five dollar bill, he wonders what would happen if one day he just said NO.

But the fantasy quickly fades as the memory of last week's bloodied nose jolts him back to reality. The bully means business. He has no other choice but to give up the cash.

Or does he?

From Prey to Princess

The United States government is ruled not by a monarchy but by a democracy. Our elected leader is the president. Over the years, several presidents have had daughters. While we don't refer to them as princesses, with the main exception of not having a birth right to rule, they are bestowed all the privileges of American "royalty."

So let's reimagine for a moment that playground scene, replacing Awkward Kid with the president's daughter.

There she is, a carefree, smartly dressed little girl; her hair is neatly brushed into two long pony tails with matching purple satin ribbons. She hovers near the merry-go-round, patiently waiting for it to slow down long enough for her to jump on and join in the fun.

Cue the bully: overgrown, ugly, and yes, still desperately in need of deodorant. He boldly saunters over to the president's daughter and whispers menacingly, "Give me your lunch...*aaaaaaaaah!*"

Before one could think twice, from behind the sliding board, two 7-foot-something men wearing dark suits and ear pieces rush in to tackle the bully, pinning him to the ground. The bully writhes in pain and begins to cry, begging for mercy. The assistant principal and teacher scurry over to be sure the president's daughter is okay.

The student body erupts into cheers! The bully, who has tormented them for months, will now be brought to justice!

Awkward Kid, still standing by the basketball court, stares in disbelief. "You've gotta be kidding me!" he mutters to himself.

What just happened here?

As a member of the first family, the president's daughter is bestowed special privileges. These include 24-hour access to members of the Secret Service whose sole purpose is to protect her from harm. They escort her everywhere she goes.

The president's daughter realizes that because of the status automatically given to her as a child of the leader of the Free World, when the bully comes along and insists that she give up her lunch money, all she must do is simply say NO.

Why?

Because she can!

Daughter of the King, if you have given your life to Christ, you too have been spiritually born into a royal family. This means that you have been granted a supernatural birth right to rule and reign in the spirit realm. You too have been afforded certain privileges simply because *you are God's child.*

The trouble is, many of us are tragically unaware of who our Heavenly Father is and the lengths to which He has gone to protect and to provide for us!

Last Will & Testament

Suppose you received this letter in the mail:

Dear (insert your name):

INTRODUCTION

I am an estate attorney representing your estranged father, who has recently passed away.

Your father was secretly a multi-billionaire and has left his entire fortune to you.

In order to collect your inheritance, you must read and follow the instructions included in this letter.

Please contact me once you have done so, and I will immediately send your payment.

Regards,

John D. Attorney

After picking yourself up off the floor and verifying that the letter was indeed legitimate, what would you do next? Would you toss the letter in the trash? Or would you put it up on a shelf, casually dismissing it? Of course not! You would probably read and re-read the letter, ensuring you understood and followed the instructions in your father's will precisely, so that you could collect the inheritance!

In reality, if you have received Jesus Christ as your Lord and Savior, you ARE the daughter of the wealthiest Father who ever lived—and still lives! *"The earth is the LORD's, and everything in it, the world, and all who live in it." (Psalm 24:1, NIV)*

He has given you access to His Perfect Last Will and Testament (both Old and New) in the Bible, the word of God. It is God's love letter to you.

Sadly, this love letter often lies on a shelf, unread and collecting dust. "I'll read it when I need it," becomes our attitude.

Precious woman of God, do you realize that the Will (of God) contains priceless principles and promises—pearls of wisdom—that are designed to make you spiritually, mentally, emotionally, physically and even financially wealthy?

"Choose my instruction rather than silver, and knowledge rather than pure gold. For wisdom is far more valuable than rubies.

Nothing you desire can compare with it." (Proverbs 8:10-11, NLT)

Do you know that there are blessings simply for reading the Will?

"Blessed is the one who reads aloud the words of this prophecy, and blessed are those who hear it and take to heart what is written in it..." (Revelation 1:3, NIV)

How it must grieve the King to know that His daughters live more like paupers than princesses, simply because we do not value our royal heritage or understand the extent of our inheritance! Yet, He extends to us daily invitations to enjoy all that He has provided (see Luke 11:15-32).

Just Say No

Make no mistake about it. The bully, whom the Bible calls the devil or Satan, is real.

While he doesn't demand money, he will boldly approach you, Princess, and snarl such profanities as, "Give me your peace of mind. Give up your hope. And while you're at it, hand over your joy." If you do not know your rights, you may quickly say, "Here you go. Take it. I *am* beginning to feel depressed and hopeless, now that you've mentioned it."

But if you've read the Will, you will be able to boldly stand up to the devil and refuse his demands, saying, "No, Satan. God has not given me a spirit of fear but of power, love and a sound mind. And I receive them in the name of Jesus." (See 2 Timothy 1:7)

Then you can collect your inheritance of peace, hope and joy knowing that the Will also says, *"Resist the devil and he will flee from you." (James 4:7b, NIV)*

And that's not all! Even when you don't have strength to resist evil, your bodyguards will handle it for you. "What bodyguards?" you ask. King David, a man after God's own heart, explains it this way:

"Surely goodness and mercy shall follow me all the days of my life..." (Psalm 23:6a, KJV)

INTRODUCTION

Daughters of the King

The purpose of **Portrait of a Princess: The Truth About You from the King's Point of View** is simple. It is designed to invite you, precious Princess, to take your rightful place in the kingdom of God.

"*...and I will dwell in the house of the Lord forever.*" *(Psalm 23:6b, KJV)*

This can only happen when you begin to understand what God says about you. You must learn the truth about who you are from the King's point of view. But most importantly, you must believe it!

Then, and only then, will you begin to experience the lavish spiritual lifestyle that God intends for you, enjoying the protected, privileged and prosperous life of a daughter of the King of Kings!

A Royal Invitation

In order to enjoy the benefits of a relationship with the King, you must first become a true Daughter of the King. There is only one road that leads to the King's palace, and that is through His son, Jesus Christ. Jesus said, "*I am the way, and the truth and the life. No man comes to the Father except through me.*" *(John 14:6 NIV)*

Jesus Christ provides eternal life and a relationship with the Father through His death on the cross and through His resurrection. "*For if, while we were God's enemies, we were reconciled to him through the death of his Son, how much more, having been reconciled, shall we be saved through his life!*" *(Romans 5:10 NIV)*

Romans 10:9 promises, "*If you confess with your mouth Jesus as Lord, and believe in your heart that God raised Him from the dead, you will be saved.*" No matter what you've done in your past, God wants you to know that He loves you and has made a way for you to have perfect fellowship with Him.

If you have never trusted in Christ as your Lord and Savior, you can do it right now. Here is a simple prayer that you can pray to express your faith and trust in Jesus:

Lord Jesus, I thank you for dying on the cross for my sins so I would have a relationship with my heavenly Father. I ask you to forgive my sins and to save me from eternal separation from God. Through faith in you, I have eternal life. Please help me to understand the privileges, promises and power you give me to live as a true daughter of the King of Kings. In Jesus' name, Amen.

If you have just prayed this prayer as an expression of your faith in Christ, congratulations! You have received Christ as your Savior and have made the best decision you will ever make—one that will change your life forever.

"But as many as received him, to them gave he power to become the [children] of God, even to them that believe on his name." (John 1:12 KJV)

Princess, welcome to the family of God! Now, let's begin our journey of discovering the promises and privileges of the Daughters of the King!

INTRODUCTION

Priceless Pearl

"We break down every thought and proud thing that puts itself up against the wisdom of God. We take hold of every thought and make it obey Christ."
1 Corinthians 10:5

Princess Proclamation

Dear Lord Jesus:
I thank You for dying on the cross for my sins so I would have a relationship with my heavenly Father.
I ask You to forgive me and to save me from eternal separation from God.
Through faith in You, I have eternal life.

*Please help me to understand the privileges, promises and power You give me to live as a true daughter of the King of Kings.
In Jesus' name. Amen.*

1

Who Do You Think You Are?

> "Stand up straight and realize who you are; that you tower over your circumstances. You are a child of God. Stand up straight!"
> –Dr. Maya Angelou

Who do you think you are?

No, really. Have you ever considered that question? Be honest. When you are alone—in the hidden, deepest, and truest parts of yourself—who do you think you are?

We are deeply driven by our sense of identity. Our feelings of value and worth for who we are is commonly known as self-esteem. It involves respect for one's self or confidence in one's own worth or abilities.

Our self-esteem evolves throughout the course of life as we develop an image of ourselves through our encounters with different people and experiences. Experiences during childhood play an especially important role in the shaping of our self-esteem. When we were growing up, the way in which we were treated by those who meant the most to us contributed significantly to the formation of our self-perception.

If, during childhood, we felt respected, considered, praised and received appropriate attention and affection, we would mostly likely develop a healthy sense of self-esteem. If, however, we were harshly criticized, abused physically, sexually or emotionally, or ignored or ridiculed, we might tend to have a lower sense of self-esteem.

An Identity Crisis

The events of our early childhood are not the only factors that can impact our feelings of self-esteem. Our successes, failures, decisions and sometimes events beyond our control can impact the way we feel about ourselves. We can be raised under the most ideal conditions and still encounter events later in life that can rattle even the strongest sense of self-worth. As a matter of fact, this is likely to occur at some point in our lives. *"Here on earth you will have many trials and sorrows,"* Jesus said. (John 16:33b, NLT)

The foundation on which we base our beliefs determines how we will survive (and even thrive) in the storms of life, which threaten what we believe to be true about ourselves.

Suppose a woman is taught from an early age to believe that her main goal in life should be to marry a successful businessman, have children and to live an extravagant lifestyle. Once she achieves those goals, her security may rest in maintaining that lifestyle, and she may find herself doing whatever it takes to keep up appearances. One day her husband comes home and tells her that he is leaving her for a younger, prettier woman. If she has defined herself as "Mrs. Successful Businessman," then when he leaves, taking his money with him, she may consider herself to be less valuable.

A man is encouraged to pursue a career as a plastic surgeon. He

Chapter One: Who Do You Think You Are?

completes his education and training, receives his credentials and begins practicing, focusing on celebrity patients. He enjoys the prestige that comes from treating his patients. One day, during surgery, one of his most famous patients dies. His career and reputation are instantly destroyed. If he has defined himself as "Celebrity M.D.," then when his reputation is ruined and his career derailed, he may consider himself to be without value.

A couple dreams of having a large family. After years of trying various methods of fertilization, they come to the realization that having a child of their own will be a dream that eludes them. If they have defined themselves as "Biological Parents," then month after month when the wife does not conceive, they may consider themselves to be failures.

These are a few

oversimplified, hypothetical examples. There are many complex life events that can shake us to our cores. They can cause us to question our value. When life does not meet our expectations, what does that say about us?

The answer depends entirely on how we define ourselves.

A common thread in each of these scenarios is that the people involved based their self-worth on changeable circumstances (i.e., marriage, money, career, family). In Matthew 7:24-27, Jesus shares a parable.

"Everyone then who hears these words of mine and does them will be like a wise man who built his house on the rock. And the rain fell, and the floods came, and the winds blew and beat on that house, but it did not fall, because it had been founded on the rock. And everyone who hears these words of mine and does not do them will be like a foolish man who built his house on the sand. And the rain fell, and the floods came, and the winds blew and beat against that house, and it fell, and great was the fall of it." (ESV)

In other words, if we want to be "unshakeable" women of God, we must define ourselves based only on what God's word says about us. This is why this book is subtitled, "The Truth about You from the King's Point of View."

God's view of us, written in His word, is the only thing that matters. Why? Because it does not change.

"The grass withers and the flowers fall, but the word of our God endures forever." (Isaiah 40:8, NIV)

"But I the LORD will speak what I will, and it shall be fulfilled without delay. For in your days, you rebellious people, I will fulfill whatever I say, declares the Sovereign LORD." (Ezekiel 12:25, NIV)

"The LORD Almighty has sworn, 'Surely, as I have planned, so it will be, and as I have purposed, so it will happen.'" (Isaiah 14:24, NIV)

Daughters of the King, we must shift from a concept of self-es-

Chapter One: Who Do You Think You Are?

teem to developing a sense of "God-esteem"—the idea that what God says to be true of us (both good and bad) is central to experiencing a life of success and spiritual prosperity.

Charm School

Many years ago, it was common for young women to attend what was known as "charm school." It was a series of classes in the social graces ranging from floral arranging to the art of serving afternoon tea. Training in etiquette, conversation and acting like a "lady" were emphasized because these skills were highly valued by society at that time.

One common exercise was designed to help the students learn to carry themselves with grace and poise. The students were required to balance a book on their heads without using their hands and to walk around the room without dropping the book. As you might imagine, this was initially an awkward exercise. At first, the book would wobble and inevitably fall. Eventually, learning to walk with the book on their heads became second nature. Once they learned to align their heads with their spines, the book was no longer at risk of falling.

Instead of a book, imagine balancing a large, ornate crown on your head—the most beautiful crown you have ever seen. As you "walk" through the chapters of **Portrait of a Princess: The Truth About You from the King's Point of View**, envision even more "jewels" of wisdom and insight being added to your crown. As you learn more about what God says about you through His word, and as you begin to appropriate that knowledge, you might sometimes feel a little awkward. You may feel unworthy to wear the crown of righteousness that God has appointed for you. But as you align your mind with His word—as you begin to believe and walk out the truth of what you learn—your crown will no longer be at risk of falling. Your acceptance of your royal heritage will become second nature.

"I rejoice in your word like one who discovers a great treasure."

(Psalm 119:162, NLT)

Daughter of the King, you will learn to wear your crown with grace and dignity, for you will begin to understand something God already knows is true about you:

"You are a chosen people, a royal priesthood, a holy nation, God's special possession, that you may declare the praises of him who called you out of darkness into his wonderful light." (1 Peter 2:9, NIV)

CHAPTER ONE: WHO DO YOU THINK YOU ARE?

Priceless Pearl

"You are a chosen people, a royal priesthood, a holy nation, God's special possession, that you may declare the praises of him who called you out of darkness into his wonderful light."
1 Peter 2:9

Princess Proclamation

Dear Heavenly Father:
I want to know who I am.
I am intrigued by the prospect that there is much more You want to share with me. Lift me from the place of my low, limited view of self-esteem, which is all about me, to Your heavenly perspective, which is unlimited and all about You.

I am Your daughter. I was created in Your image to do unlimited, impossible things for Your glory.

When You show me something that displeases You, help me to humble myself and correct it right away. Encourage my heart by showing me when I'm on the right path.

I acknowledge that without You, I can do nothing.

I am ready to learn more about who I am from the only perspective that truly matters—Yours. Now reveal my true identity in You.

In Jesus' name. Amen.

CHAPTER ONE: WHO DO YOU THINK YOU ARE?

COULD IT BE?

Could it be there's a Princess who lives within me?
Could it be?
And does she ever wonder who I am?
Will we meet?
Did she read my story? Can she tell if it ends happily?
Could it be there's a Princess within me?

Could it be there's a Princess who lives within me?
Could it be?
Why does she feel unworthy to be called royalty?
Could she please give a sign if this is not a fantasy?
Could it be there's a Princess within me?

Could it be there's a Princess who lives within me (living in me)?
Why does she feel unworthy to be called royalty?
Did she read my story? Does it end happily?

Could it be there's a Princess?
Finally, can we solve this mystery?
Is there a Princess within me?

2

A King's Ransom

"It is for freedom that Christ has set us free. Stand firm, then, and do not let yourselves be burdened again by a yoke of slavery."
—Galatians. 5:1, NIV

They stood in the middle of the vast fields, surveying the fluffy, white blooms neatly arranged in rows as far as the eye could see. In just a few short weeks, it would be harvest time. Men, women with newborns tied to their backs and young children alike sweltered in the Galveston heat and humidity as they used their hoes to clear the rows of grass and weeds so that only the tender cotton plants remained.

They labored, trailed by a whip-yielding overseer on horseback. One slave led the group, a row or two ahead. If someone worked faster than the leader, he was whipped. If another fell behind or took even a moment to rest, she too would be beaten mercilessly. The hoeing and lashing continued in this way, from dawn to dusk, until

Chapter Two: A King's Ransom

the back-breaking work was completed.

One day, as they toiled in the fields, a cloud of dust arose in the distance. The rhythmic thud of horses' hooves and the blaring of bugles grew louder as the troops advanced. They all stood motionless as the overseer lit from his horse and walked out to meet the Union soldiers.

Soon, they heard the urgent news General Granger's regiment came to deliver:

"The people of Texas are informed that in accordance with a proclamation from the Executive of the United States, all slaves are free. This involves an absolute equality of personal rights and rights of property between former masters and slaves, and the connection heretofore existing between them becomes that between employer and free laborer."

All slaves are free.

Free?

The words hung in the air like the limp, lifeless bodies of runaway slaves who had been captured and lynched in the town square.

Two and a half years earlier, in January of 1863, President Abraham Lincoln had signed the Emancipation Proclamation, an executive order freeing the slaves in the United States. The Emancipation Proclamation had little impact on Texans, however, because of the limited number of troops in place to enforce the order. But with the surrender of General Lee in April of 1865, and the arrival of General Granger's regiment, the forces were finally strong enough to overcome the opposition.

Imagine, for a moment, the wave of emotions that must have washed over the people. From jubilation (*We are finally free!*) to fear (*Where will we go? How will we live?*) to seething anger (*Two and a half years of our precious freedom has been wasted!*).

Today, each year on the 19th day of June, "Juneteenth" is recognized in many American cities in commemoration of the ending of slavery. It is a bittersweet reminder of the deception the Galveston slaves experienced, long after they were legally freed from bondage.

Although Jesus Christ died to set us free from the power of sin over our lives, many of God's daughters remain spiritually and mentally enslaved. We live as though sin is still our overseer.

The word of God teaches that through the original man, Adam, the human race was born into sin.

"Therefore, just as sin entered the world through one man, and death through sin, and in this way death came to all people, because all sinned." (Romans 5:12, NIV)

As a result, we became separated from God and enslaved to sin because of our disobedient hearts that had defiantly turned away from God.

"Jesus replied, 'Very truly I tell you, everyone who sins is a slave to sin.'" (John 8:34, NIV)

When Satan says, "Jump!" we ask, "How high?" The slightest influence, pressures, and difficulties can cause us to respond in patterns established in our flesh long before we came to know Christ. We continue to follow the devil's orders simply because we do not understand what Christ's death means for our freedom.

Unable to free ourselves from sin's control, our only hope was a Redeemer who, as *"the Word [who] became flesh" (John 1:14)*, could Himself become the divine Emancipation Proclamation and decree our spiritual freedom with ultimate authority and finality.

Christ, Our Redeemer

"Redemption involves recovering something by paying the debt against it. A redeemer is one who buys back, or pays ransom, or makes amends." —Walter L. Thompson

"Or do you not know that your body is the temple of the Holy Spirit who is in you, whom you have from God, and you are not your own? For you were bought at a price; therefore glorify God in your body and in your spirit, which are God's." (1 Corinthians 6:19-20, NKJV)

When Jesus Christ died on the cross and was raised from the dead more than two thousand years ago, He redeemed us from the slave market of sin.

In order to better understand and appreciate the concept of spiritual redemption, it is helpful to look at the historical context of slavery in biblical times. There are several different words in the Greek language (the original language of the New Testament) that define redemption.

💎 *Agorazo:* to buy or sell in the marketplace (see 1 Corinthians 6:20)

💎 *Exagorazo:* to buy out from the marketplace; to purchase slaves from a slave market (see Galatians 3:13)

💎 *Apolutrosis:* to buy back a slave, thus making him free by payment of a ransom (see Romans 3:24)

💎 *Lutron:* a ransom price paid in order to free a slave (see Matthew 20:28)

Slaves in the ancient world were sold in the *agora*, a market place. An Israelite who had to sell himself into slavery because of poverty could be redeemed by a close relative. If the relative was willing and able to pay off their debt, they could go to the agora, pay the price for that slave, and set him free.

This is redemption: freedom by payment of a price. This is what the Lord Jesus Christ did for us when He was crucified, was buried and rose again.

Christ was in all ways qualified to redeem us. In Leviticus 25:47-49, God laid out the conditions of the law of redemption:

1. **The Redeemer must be next of kin.**

Jesus Christ is the son of God. When we accept Him as our Lord and Savior, the Bible tells us that we are, at that very moment, spiritually adopted as sons (and daughters) of God.

"God decided in advance to adopt us into his own family by

bringing us to himself through Jesus Christ. This is what he wanted to do, and it gave him great pleasure." (Ephesians 1:5, NLT).

"The Spirit you received does not make you slaves, so that you live in fear again; rather, the Spirit you received brought about your adoption to sonship. And by him we cry, 'Abba, Father.'" (Romans 8:15, NIV)

Scripture makes it clear that those who have received Christ are spiritual "siblings" with Christ (the Son of God) and therefore, spiritually next of kin.

2. The Redeemer must be able to pay the price fully.

In the Old Testament, offerings and sacrifices were a key part of the practice of relationship with God. Although sacrifices were offered to God for many purposes, they were often offered to atone for the sin of the people. The sin (or purification) offering was the means through which worshipers could receive forgiveness for their sins.

"Make an altar of earth for me and sacrifice on it your burnt offerings and fellowship offerings, your sheep and goats and your cattle. Wherever I cause my name to be honored, I will come to you and bless you." (Exodus 20:24, NIV)

The Old Testament outlines very detailed rules for the people of God to follow during this ritual procedure. One of those requirements was that the animal to be sacrificed must be a young healthy male, without spot or blemish, of the highest quality available to the offender (see Leviticus 18:20-22).

"*For God made Christ, who never sinned, to be the offering for our sin, so that we could be made right with God through Christ.*" *(2 Corinthians 5:21, NLT).*

Because of Christ's sacrifice, we are no longer required to offer animal sacrifices for our sin (see Hebrews chapter 9). God accepts the substitutionary death of Jesus alone to atone for our sins through our faith in Christ.

Jesus, "*the Lamb of God who takes away the sins of the world*" *(John 1:29),* was perfectly qualified to pay the full price for our sins.

3. The Redeemer must be willing to pay the price.

Jesus willingly laid down His life as a sacrifice for the sins of the world.

"*I am the good shepherd; I know my sheep and my sheep know me—just as the Father knows me and I know the Father—and I lay down my life for the sheep...The reason my Father loves me is that I lay down my life—only to take it up again. No one takes it from me, but I lay it down of my own accord. I have authority to lay it down and authority to take it up again. This command I received from my Father.*" *(John 10:14-15, 17-18, NIV)*

Once we were purchased out of the slave market, God began to unveil His new purpose for us.

"*And that is what some of you were. But you were washed, you were sanctified, you were justified in the name of the Lord Jesus Christ and by the Spirit of our God.*" *(1 Corinthians 6:11, NIV)*

"*For God knew his people in advance, and he chose them to become like his Son, so that his Son would be the firstborn among many brothers and sisters. And having chosen them, he called them to come to him. And having called them, he gave them right standing with himself. And having given them right standing, he* gave them his glory." (Romans 8:29-30, NLT)

Christ, Our Ruler

Before we begin to explore the thoughts of the King (see Jeremiah 29:11) concerning His daughters in the chapters to follow, we must be properly introduced to Him. We need to understand more about who He is and why He is worthy of our total praise and dedication. This understanding will begin to transform everything you ever thought you understood about God and will cause you to have a deeper love and appreciation for what He has done on your behalf.

The whole of scripture establishes Jesus Christ as Ruler of a spiritual kingdom. There are dozens of references to the kingship of Christ, though this chapter highlights but a few.

Beginning in the Old Testament, Christ is foreshadowed as the coming King (see Psalms 24:7-10).

As we fast forward through the gospels in the New Testament, we find Matthew tracing Jesus' family tree, highlighting His royal lineage as son of David. *"In Bethlehem in Judea,"* they replied, *"for this is what the prophet has written: 'But you, Bethlehem, in the land of Judah, are by no means least among the rulers of Judah; for out of you will come a ruler who will shepherd my people Israel.'"* (Matthew 2:5-6, NIV).

Christ Himself claimed to be king, speaking of His kingdom and equating it with the kingdom of God. *"The Son of Man will send out his angels, and they will weed out of his kingdom everything that causes sin and all who do evil. They will throw them into the blazing furnace, where there will be weeping and gnashing of teeth. Then the righteous will shine like the sun in the kingdom of their Father."* (Matthew 13:41-43a, NIV).

And even in His final hours as He hung on a cross, the dying thief beside Him pleads, *"Jesus, remember me when you come into your kingdom."* (Luke 23:42-43, NIV). Jesus' response affirms His royal position when He answers, *"Truly I tell you, today you will be with me in paradise."*

Thy Kingdom Come

When Jesus rose from the dead, God appointed Him over all human authority, including the rulers of the earth. What an amazing thought! Jesus is alive today presiding from heaven over the kings of the earth!

"Who, being in very nature God, did not consider equality with God something to be used to his own advantage; rather, he made himself nothing by taking the very nature of a servant, being made in human likeness. And being found in appearance as a man, he humbled himself by becoming obedient to death—even death on a cross! Therefore God exalted him to the highest place and gave him the name that is above every name, that at the name of Jesus every knee should bow, in heaven and on earth and under the earth and every tongue acknowledge that Jesus Christ is Lord, to the glory of God the Father." (Philippians 2:6-11, NIV)

Since Christ has all authority in heaven and on earth, this means that we who believe on His name have become citizens of His heavenly kingdom.

"All authority in heaven and on earth has been given to me. Therefore, go and make disciples of all nations." (Matthew 28:18b-19, NIV)

"But our citizenship is in heaven. And we eagerly await a Savior from there, the Lord Jesus Christ." (Philippians 3:20, NIV)

Christ's Kingdom Lies Within

Not only has Christ been given dominion to rule the earth, but on a personal level, He wants to be Ruler of every aspect of our spiritual and physical lives. He cannot be Ruler or "Lord" of part. His sacrificial, atoning death has earned Him the right to master every area concerning us.

Just as we once lived as slaves to sin, Christ has redeemed us so that we can live as servants of a loving, compassionate King who wants to give us the best life possible.

"*Christ has freed us so that we may enjoy the benefits of freedom. Therefore, be firm [in this freedom], and don't become slaves again.*" *(Galatians 5:1, GWT)*

When we truly begin to yield lordship of Jesus Christ, we will want to obey Him completely, wholeheartedly, and without reservation. When Christ is the Lord of your life, you will begin to develop a heart and mind that desires to do what He tells you to do—the mind and heart of Christ (see 1 Corinthians 2:16).

"*What? Know ye not that your body is the temple of the Holy Ghost which is in you, which ye have of God, and ye are not your own? For ye are bought with a price: therefore glorify God in your body, and in your spirit, which are God's.*" *(1 Corinthians 6:19-20, KJV)*

Christ, Our Righteousness

When Satan was our overseer and sin separated us from God, we needed a way back to Him. Christ's redemption allows us direct access to God.

"*For there is one God and one mediator between God and mankind, the man Christ Jesus, who gave himself as a ransom for all people.*" *(1 Peter 2:5-6a, NIV)*

God is holy and requires holiness. Holiness means to be different and set apart for a special purpose. "*For it is written: 'Be holy, because I am holy.'*" *(1 Peter 1:16, NIV)* But how can a holy God relate to humans who were born into sin? Even our best efforts at perfection are not good enough in God's eyes.

"*All of us have become like one who is unclean; and all our righteous acts are like filthy rags.*" *(Isaiah 64:6a, NIV)*.

"*For all have sinned and fall short of the glory of God.*" *(Romans 3:23, NIV)*

In addition to experiencing the forgiveness that God provides through the blood of Jesus, we also must be covered with a righteousness that is acceptable to God.

Think of it this way: If we liken forgiveness to taking a shower, then righteousness is the equivalent of getting dressed. When we get dirty, we shower. Afterward, we dress to cover our nakedness and to be appropriately presentable before others.

When we pray to God or enjoy fellowship with Him, we are, in a sense, coming into His presence. And when we think about coming into the presence of a holy God, we realize that we must be clothed in a way that impresses Him. We must be clothed with a righteousness that is acceptable to God—the righteousness of Christ.

In the classic hymn, "The Solid Rock," Lyricist Edward Mote expresses this beautifully as he writes, "Dressed in His righteousness alone, faultless to stand before the throne."

"God made him who had no sin to be sin for us, so that in him we might become the righteousness of God." (2 Corinthians 5:21, NIV)

Now, God sees us not as we are in our sinfulness, but in Christ. Jesus is our perfect standing before God. It is only the righteousness of Christ that can possibly satisfy the perfect demand of God's holiness.

"Now all of us can come to the Father through the same Holy Spirit because of what Christ has done for us." (Ephesians 2:18, NLT)

It is only by grace—God's unmerited, undeserved favor— that we become partakers of the glorious gifts of salvation, forgiveness and righteousness. And because we know we are undeserving, we must give God all the glory for them.

"For by grace you have been saved through faith; and that not of yourselves, it is the gift of God; not as a result of works, so that no one may boast." (Ephesians 2:8-9, NIV).

Priceless Pearl

"It is for freedom that Christ has set us free. Stand firm, then, and do not let yourselves be burdened again by a yoke of slavery."
Galatians. 5:1

Princess Proclamation

Dear Heavenly Father:
What great love You've shown in providing a Redeemer for me!
I was a slave to sin and had no way to free myself. Because of Your love, I am no longer enslaved. I choose to live for You. Help me to live in the complete freedom that You have provided.
When I am tempted to return to old mindsets and behaviors, remind me of the precious gift of Your Son, Jesus, and what He means

for my future. Help me not to take this precious gift for granted.

I am Yours. No more a slave to sin but a servant of the Most High God.

For this gift of freedom, I give you praise.

In Jesus' name. Amen.

THE COLOR OF KINGS

There was a time when master fishermen would travel out to sea
In search of treasure so unusual the world had never seen.
And they would cast their nets to gather in a shell so highly prized.
Caught so that queens and kings could wear the things only royalty could buy.

But first...

It had to be crushed. When broken by blows
Out of the fragments ink would flow.
What a sacrifice! Such a great price was paid indeed.
The linen was plunged and when it was raised
All of its color was displayed.
It had to be crushed
So they could wear purple
The color of kings.

So many times the Master taught the crowds which gathered by the sea.

Chapter Two: A King's Ransom

In search of words of life they treasured from the Man of Galilee.
And as they cast their cares and gathered there with yearning in their eyes;
So unaware that in their midst was One who would come to pay the price.

But first...

He had to be crushed and broken by blows.
While nailed to the cross His blood did flow.
What a sacrifice! Such a great price was paid indeed.
Though plunged in a grave, when He was raised
All of His power was displayed.
He had to be crushed
So they could wear purple,
The color of kings.

He had to be crushed. He had to be pressed.
So that my life could now be blessed.
What a sacrifice! For such a great price was paid for me!
Though plunged in a grave, when He was raised
All of His power was displayed.
He had to be crushed.
He had to be crushed.
My savior was crushed
So I could wear purple...the color of kings.

3

The Purpose of a Princess

"It's in Christ that we find out who we are and what we are living for."
—Ephesians 1:11, MSG

"You were not created to conform. You were not created to compare. You were not created to compete. You were not created to compromise. You were created to contribute to God's kingdom and make a significant difference with your life."
—Erik Rees

"It's not about you."

The first four words of the best-selling hardback in modern literary history, Pastor Rick Warren's "Purpose Driven Life," succinctly answer the cry of every woman's heart: "Why was I created?"

What makes me unique—different from any woman who has lived before or will come after me? What makes me valuable? What

CHAPTER THREE: THE PURPOSE OF A PRINCESS

is my reason for living?

The King desires that His daughters understand His larger purpose for creating us as women. He wants us to discover His specific, unique purpose for our individual lives. In other words, what purpose will go unachieved in this world if you do not personally accomplish it?

What an amazing, sobering thought! Out of the billions of women alive today in the world, could there actually be a void that only you can fill?

Yes!

"For we are God's handiwork, created in Christ Jesus to do good works, which God prepared in advance for us to do." (Ephesians 2:10, NIV)

God has specifically designed and prepared you, Princess, even before you were born, to accomplish good in the lives of those He has placed around you at this precise moment in time.

"My frame was not hidden from you when I was made in the secret place, when I was woven together in the depths of the earth. Your eyes saw my unformed body; all the days ordained for me were written in your book before one of them came to be." (Psalm 139:15-16, NIV)

It brings God glory when we discover what we were born to do and when we obediently carry out His mission in our lifetimes.

Understanding God's specific purpose for your life will take some soul-searching. It will take prayer, evaluation and assessment of your natural and spiritual gifts, talents, desires, abilities and resources. And guess what? You can expect your understanding of God's purpose to change several times over the course of your lifetime. There is no single thing that God has called us to do. We have many different roles and "talents," and God expects us to invest them all in the lives of others (see Matthew 25:14-30).

The various seasons of our lives will dictate how those roles may change and how our talents and gifts will be used. We can work out

God's purposes for our lives in many different ways that will impact people for God's glory.

While this book does not delve into the specifics of how to determine your spiritual gifts and your calling, there are many excellent resources specifically designed to help women of faith discover how they might best serve others as members of the body of Christ.

However, it is necessary to develop a clear sense of why you were created so that you will come to value your own unique life experiences. When we do not understand the value God places on our lives and our unique purposes, we can become envious of others, discontent with our own lives, and end up being void of all hope for the future.

"For you created my inmost being; you knit me together in my mother's womb. I praise you because I am fearfully and wonderfully made; your works are wonderful, I know that full well." (Psalm 139:13-14, NIV)

The Princess is a work in progress

"The Lord will perfect that which concerns me; Your mercy, O Lord, endures forever; do not forsake the works of Your hands." (Psalm 138:8, NKJV)

As women, we can be very critical of ourselves and each other. Instead of celebrating what is good about us and others, we can often focus on flaws and imperfections. This causes us to become discontent, critical, envious and bitter (see Proverbs 14:30).

"We do not dare to classify or compare ourselves with some who commend themselves. When they measure themselves by themselves and compare themselves with themselves, they are not wise." (2 Corinthians 10:12, NIV)

In other words, when we make ourselves or others the standard of perfection, we and they will always come up short. There will always be someone who is smarter, richer, more accomplished, prettier, more physically fit, more talented…the list goes on. While there are certainly some practical things we can and should do to improve our lives and become the best women we can be, we must remember that God alone is the standard of perfection. We must learn to embrace who we are right now because in God's eyes, we have always been more than enough.

"...Be relaxed with what you have. Since God assured us, 'I'll never let you down, never walk off and leave you,' we can boldly quote, God is there, ready to help; I'm fearless no matter what. Who or what can get to me?" (Hebrews 13:5-6, MSG)

God knows we are far from perfect. As a matter of fact, the Bible compares all of our self-proclaimed goodness and beauty to filthy, nasty rags (see Isaiah 64:6). But God never required perfection in order to bless us. He simply requires a willing and obedient heart to do what He says (see Isaiah 1:19).

We are accepted into God's royal family when we receive the gift of salvation through His son, Christ Jesus. It is the finished work of the Holy Spirit alone which brings about lasting change in us. If we are willing and patient participants in that process, we will begin to witness the amazing spiritual transformation God has planned for our lives.

"Being confident of this very thing, that he which hath begun a good work in you will perform it until the day of Jesus Christ." (Philippians 1:6, KJV)

The Princess is a reflection of her father, the King

From the cleft of my chin to my slightly crooked smile — even the shape of my legs comes from my Daddy. Through the years, my mother has often joked that Daddy could never deny that I was his child (not that the thought ever crossed his mind). "You look just like your Daddy," she would often say. Those words gave me a sense of belonging; a "knowing" that I had a heritage to which I could connect.

"But there were people who did believe in his name. They did re-

ceive him. He gave all those who received him and believed him the right to become children of God. They were born into God's family by God. That is, they were not born into his family in the way a person is born into this world. It was not by any person's will." (John 1:12-13, WE)

Those who have received Christ have been spiritually born into God's family. Our heavenly Father expects His children to look like Him. The more time we spend with Him in prayer and in reading His word, the more we will begin to think, speak and act like Him. We will begin to "look" like Him. This pleases God. It's the reason He created us in the first place.

"Then God said, "Let us make mankind in our image, in our likeness, so that they may rule..." (Genesis 1:26a, NIV)

"So God created mankind in his own image, in the image of God he created them; male and female he created them." (Genesis 1:27, NIV)

"For those God foreknew he also predestined to be conformed to the image of his Son, that he might be the firstborn among many brothers and sisters." (Romans 8:29, NIV)

God has many ways of conforming us to the image of Christ. The Bible refers to the process of refining gold and silver as an illustration of how God sometimes uses the heat of difficulty and trials to make us look more like Him. Author, June Hunt, explains this process beautifully in "A Letter from June on Trials."

Our King is a Refiner who uses the heat of trials and difficulties to purify our hearts. Once the natural ore is broken up, the Refiner places the ore into a fireproof melting pot where other metals that would mar the quality of the gold or silver are removed. Proverbs 17:3 says, "The crucible for silver and the furnace for gold, but the Lord tests the heart." (NIV)

Once the ore is melted, the Refiner then begins the process of skimming off the dross, a layer of impurities that forms on the surface of the hot liquid metal. Dross represents anything ungodly or

Chapter Three: The Purpose of a Princess

unholy that would keep us from being like Christ. It can take several turns in the fire to produce purified gold or silver.

The Refiner continues to remove the dross, leaving behind shimmering gold and silver more pure and precious than before. To gauge his progress, He looks for his own reflection on the surface. Only when the Refiner looks into the crucible and sees a clear reflection of himself is the process complete. It is then that the gold or silver attains its highest degree of purity. Isaiah 48:10 says, *"See, I have refined you, though not as silver; I have tested you in the furnace of affliction."* (NIV)

God can use our challenges to shape us into the women He has called us to be. As we grow and develop in Him, we will begin to hear Him speaking softly to our hearts, *"You are altogether beautiful, my darling, and there is no blemish in you."* (Song of Solomon 4:7, NASB)

The princess is a priceless work of art

"What makes a great collector great is his or her ability to separate out specific works of art from the millions of pieces already

in existence and assemble them in such a way as to increase or advance our understanding of that art in particular or of the evolution of art in general." —Alan Bamberger, fine art consultant and appraiser

"For we are God's masterpiece. He has created us anew in Christ Jesus, so that we can do the good things he planned for us long ago." (Ephesians 2:10, NLT)

God, the Master Artist, intentionally created you by divine design and chose you to be a member of His family. In the beginning, God created the earth, animals, and mankind. Even after having created all of those wonderful things, God knew that something was still missing. Woman was God's last creation—His pièce de résistance.

You are God's masterpiece—His crown jewel; His finest work of art—created specifically in His image. God designed you to be a reflection of Him. Even with all of your flaws, imperfections and past mistakes, you were created purely for His enjoyment!

"You are worthy, O Lord our God, to receive glory and honor and power. For you created all things, and they exist because you created what you pleased." (Revelation 4:11, NLT)

Daughter of the King, prized possession of the Most High God, you must know that you have been hand-selected to reflect God's light, grace and love to the world.

"But you are a chosen race, a royal priesthood, a holy nation, a people for God's own possession, so that you may proclaim the excellencies of Him who has called you out of darkness into His marvelous light." (1 Peter 2:9, NASB)

May you shine more and more beautifully as God's precious work of art as you come to understand the great love and admiration He has for you!

CHAPTER THREE: THE PURPOSE OF A PRINCESS

Priceless Pearl

"For we are God's masterpiece. He has created us anew in Christ Jesus, so that we can do the good things he planned for us long ago."
Ephesians 2:10

Princess Proclamation

Dear Heavenly Father:

When I think about how I was created in Your image—solely for Your pleasure—I am amazed!

I sometimes feel so unworthy and inadequate. In those moments, help me remember that You said I am a masterpiece, hand designed by you, for a specific purpose that only I can fill. You will *give me strength and courage to accomplish that purpose.*

Now, help me understand my purpose, day by day. With each new encounter, show me what You want me to do or say, so that I can bring You glory. Purify me. Remove anything from my heart that is not like You. I want the world to see Your light shining through me.

In Jesus' name. Amen.

CHAPTER THREE: THE PURPOSE OF A PRINCESS

Lyrical Love Letter

IN HIS EYES

He'd walk through the door with his arms open wide.
When I would run over he'd lift me up high.
He'd spin me around and I'd laugh 'til I cried.
'Cause I was Daddy's girl. He was my world.

Then Mama would say, "Babe, you're spoiling that child."
And he'd shrug his shoulders and flash her a smile.
We'd go off to my room where we'd play for a while.
Though I was small, still I recall.

His eyes would wink at me playfully.
His eyes would glare as he scolded me.
But the look on his face told me time can't erase
All the love my Daddy had for me.
In his eyes he saw what I couldn't see.
For his eyes saw only the best in me.
Then he'd call me his princess; he sure was my king.
Oh, I loved the way he looked at me.

The days turned to months and the months into years.
We shared precious moments of laughter and tears.
And whenever I needed him he would be near.
'Cause I was Daddy's girl. He was my world.
And when the time came to spread my wings and fly.
He said, "Try and fail. But don't dare fail to try;
Remember your name and true love never dies."
Still, through it all, do you know what I recall?

His eyes grew dim as the years would pass.
But his eyes still burned with a love that lasts.
As his hands stroked my cheek, oh, for hours we'd speak
Of the hopes and dreams he had for me.
In his eyes I could do what could not be done.
In his eyes I could stand when I'd want to run.
Though my Ddaddy is gone, still his words carry on.
How I miss the way he looked at me!

And as I've grown older, this world has grown colder.
I still can hear him say,
"It's not about what you do, but how God looks at you."
And my fears begin to melt away.

For in God's eyes I can do what cannot be done.
In His eyes I can stand when I want to run.
When I look on His face I know time can't erase
All the love the Father has for me.
And His eyes can see what I cannot see.
For His eyes see only the best in me.
Yes, He calls me His Princess, for he is my King.
And it's changed the way I look at me.
Now, I see…

Chapter Three: The Purpose of a Princess

Through His eyes.

Heavenly Father, help my sisters see through Your eyes.

4

The Preparation of a Princess

> "So will the King desire your beauty; because He is your Lord, be submissive and reverence and honor Him."
> —Psalm 45:11, AMPC

> "Charm can mislead and beauty soon fades. The woman to be admired and praised is the woman who lives in the fear of God."
> —Proverbs 31:30, MSG

A hush falls over the room. As she enters, all conversation ceases, for words fail to describe the splendor of the woman who has just captivated the crowd.

Bathed in beauty. Dripping in jewels. Her flawless frame is covered in couture. Perfumed by the finest fragrance money can buy, her graceful steps are hardly noticed. She glides as if her perfectly pedicured feet were instead wheels.

Halle. Lena. Liz. Grace. Audrey. Iman. If you could clone these

Chapter Four: The Preparation of a Princess

classic beauties and combine them to create one fabulous, flawless woman, she would still have nothing on this queen.

For the past year, she's been preparing for this moment—the moment when she would be called into the king's chambers. She was handpicked for this mission. She's studied what to say, how to look, and how to act and has risen to the top of her class. She is the cream of the crop.

Still, she's nervous. Worry floods her mind. *What if he is angry that I disturbed him? What if he sends me away? Even worse, what if he has me killed?* But as she recalls the passionate pleas of her beloved uncle and the perilous plight of her people, she steels herself. This is her moment—her time to make the difference she alone was born to make. She knows she was specially designed "for such a time as this."

Her name? Esther.

Full of mystery, espionage, murderous plots and romance, her story (which reads more like a best-selling novel) is told in her namesake book in the Bible. It is the story of how one woman's incredible faith, unparalleled beauty, wisdom, loyalty, and bravery in the face of death were used by God to save an entire nation from destruction.

How did she do it?

Although she was not born into royalty, she was chosen by God and was prepared to step into the royal role He had selected her even before her birth. Part of this preparation involved purification and pampering.

"Before a young woman's turn came to go in to King Xerxes, she had to complete twelve months of beauty treatments prescribed for the women, six months with oil of myrrh and six with perfumes and cosmetics." (Esther 2:12, NIV)

She learned how to enhance her natural beauty in ways that pleased the king and gave her access to him. This resulted in her being chosen as queen and put her in a position to use her God-given gifts for a higher purpose.

Princess, you too, have been born with a wealth of spiritual assets that can and should be enhanced in ways that please the King. When we cultivate these assets, God will place us in positions of influence and will give us the wisdom and courage to carry out our unique purposes as princesses in our respective royal realms.

Extreme Spiritual Makeover

"What matters is not your outer appearance—the styling of your hair, the jewelry you wear, the cut of your clothes—but your inner disposition. Cultivate inner beauty, the gentle, gracious kind that God delights in. The holy women of old were beautiful before God that way..." (1 Peter 3:3-5b, MSG)

"Extreme Makeover" was a popular television program which aired in 2002. People from all across America volunteered to receive extensive makeovers involving plastic surgery, cosmetic dentistry, intense exercise regimens, and hair and wardrobe styling. Though their processes varied, each participant had the same goal in mind: to improve what they perceived as physical flaws that somehow diminished their sense of self-worth and their quality of life. These makeovers were always dramatic and life-changing. The participants seemed to have been given a new lease on life once they saw the "new and improved" versions of themselves.

While the success of the series served to boost the clientele of plastic surgeons and cosmetic dentists across America, it also had a larger impact on the millions of viewers who faithfully watched the series. It spawned copycat extreme weight-loss shows and influenced America's fixation on exercise, clean eating, juicing, physical appearance and personal style.

The popularity of "selfies" today is also having a huge impact on the facial plastic surgery industry. According to one recent study, one in three facial plastic surgeons surveyed saw an increase in requests for procedures due to patients being more self-aware of their looks on social media. In fact, the surgeons noted increased photo sharing and patients' dissatisfaction with their own image on social media sites as a rising trend.

"Social platforms like Instagram [and] Snapchat...which are solely image-based, force patients to hold a microscope up to their own image and often look at it with a more self-critical eye than ever before," said American Academy of Facial Plastic and Reconstructive Surgery President, Dr. Edward Farrior. "These images are often the first impressions young people put out there to prospective friends, romantic interests and employers, and our patients want to put their best face forward."

But with so much focus on physical appearance, how much attention do we place on spiritual beauty and fitness, which God says is much more important?

"The LORD doesn't see things the way you see them. People judge by outward appearance, but the LORD looks at the heart." (1 Samuel 16:7b, NLT)

There are many areas of our lives that are in need of spiritual reconstruction and enhancement. It is crucial that we become aware of our spiritual flaws so that God can develop us and use us to our highest potential in Him.

The Eyes Have It

"Be not wise in thine own eyes: fear the LORD, and depart from evil." (Proverbs 3:7, KJV)

"Every way of a man is right in his own eyes: but the LORD pondereth the hearts." (Proverbs 21:2, KJV)

People who wear corrective lenses or are visually impaired understand the frustration of not having 20/20 vision. Sometimes, they are restricted from clearly seeing objects that are either too close or too far away. Others may not be able to see well at night. Whatever the problem, perfect vision eludes them and causes a constant sense of frustration. No wonder laser eye surgery is one of the most commonly requested cosmetic surgeries!

Spiritually speaking, each of us faces a similar problem. We often lack spiritual vision, unable to figure out God's will for our lives. So we stumble along, making foolish decisions, instead of seeking the Lord for His divine direction. Or if we do ask for help, we become impatient in waiting for God's response. Even worse, we sometimes reject godly counsel if it's not what we wanted to hear.

"And even when you ask, you don't get it because your motives are all wrong—you want only what will give you pleasure." (James 4:3, NLT)

God promised that if we trust Him wholeheartedly, relying on His wisdom, He will give us direction (see Proverbs 3:5,6). This is part of the process of submitting to the lordship of Christ in our lives.

We never need to stumble along blindly, fumbling our way through life, when the King stands ready to order our every step and to correct our spiritual blindness, replacing it with perfect vision.

"Open my eyes to see the wonderful truths in your instructions. Turn my eyes from worthless things, and give me life through your word." (Psalm 119:18, 37, NLT)

"Mine eyes are ever toward the LORD; for he shall pluck my feet out of the net." (Psalm 25:15, KJV)

Watch Your Mouth!

Invisible braces. Porcelain veneers. Dental implants. It's amazing what dental surgeons can do to dramatically improve a person's appearance by whitening or straightening their teeth. Crooked or missing teeth can often be fixed with just a few procedures.

As Daughters of the King, we also need to focus on improving our mouths. The damage we can do with our words is astonishing. Sometimes we gossip, offer a critical opinion, or degrade others simply because we've given no thought to the power of our words, nor have we given control of our mouths to the Holy Spirit.

"The tongue has the power of life and death, and those who love

Chapter Four: The Preparation of a Princess

it will eat its fruit." (Proverbs 18:21, NIV)

"Let the words of my mouth, and the meditation of my heart, be acceptable in thy sight, O LORD, my strength, and my redeemer." (Psalm 19:14, KJV)

But we must also be aware of the things we say to and about ourselves. We can often be our own greatest enemies in this area. Negative self-talk ("I hate myself. I'm so stupid. I can't seem to get anything right. I will never/always be...") is so damaging to our self-worth! Our speech must echo what God says.

"For I know the plans I have for you," declares the LORD, "plans to prosper you and not to harm you, plans to give you hope and a future." (Jeremiah 29:11, NIV)

The Bible says that we should use our mouths to lift others up, to heal wounds, and to share the good news of the salvation of our Lord and Savior, Jesus Christ (see Proverbs 31:26). Instead, we often speak with evil intentions and outcomes (see James 3:5-12). We need to pray that the Lord would set a watch over our mouths so that whatever we say will draw others to Christ, not injure them and push them further away from the blessing that God has for them.

Let's be sure to ask the Holy Spirit to purify and straighten our words so that we are as attractive to Him and to others as we can possibly be.

"My mouth would encourage you and comfort from my lips would bring you relief." (Job 16:5, NIV)

"All the words of my mouth are in righteousness; there is nothing forward or perverse in them." (Proverbs 8:8, KJV)

Follow Your Nose

The majority of women and men who sought elective plastic surgery last year were dissatisfied with their noses. Why? Perhaps it's because the nose is one of the most prominent facial features. You can't hide or disguise it. You either love it or hate it. And most of those who had plastic surgery decided the latter.

Noses serve a number of purposes. They help shape facial contour. They serve as the primary conduit for breathing. They provide the only means we have to smell. If you lost this function, you would lose a primary means of determining your surroundings without relying on your sight or hearing. And think about how many things can be smelled but not seen (like harmful gasses).

Your sense of smell provides you with a crucial sense of direction. Sometimes, we have a hard time discerning and understanding our surroundings. Or we simply ignore signs that the Lord has obviously placed in our paths. But if we develop a sensitivity to the leading of the Holy Spirit, we won't miss out on the directions he places "right under our noses."

"He that followeth after righteousness and mercy findeth life, righteousness, and honour." (Proverbs 21:21, KJV)

"Beloved, follow not that which is evil, but that which is good. He that doeth good is of God: but he that doeth evil hath not seen God." (3 John 1:11, KJV)

Matters of the Heart

High blood pressure. High cholesterol. Fatty foods. These are a few of the culprits that contribute to heart disease. And if we don't incorporate regular exercise into our routines, we set ourselves up for the possibility of heart problems later in life.

But when we speak of the heart in spiritual terms, it is the center of our mind, will and emotions. It is our spirit. It is the place where the Holy Spirit resides.

The word of God speaks clearly on this subject. Consider Jeremiah 17:9. *"The heart is deceitful above all things, and it is exceedingly perverse and corrupt and severely, mortally sick! Who can know it [perceive, understand, be acquainted with his own heart and mind]?" (AMP)*

In verse 10 of the same chapter, hear the King's warning concerning our hearts:

Chapter Four: The Preparation of a Princess

"I the LORD search the heart and examine the mind, to reward each person according to their conduct, according to what their deeds deserve." (Jeremiah 17:10, NIV)

No matter how pure we think our intentions, God knows that we tend to seek after those things that gratify our desires. And if we would be honest, we would have to admit that we often choose to please ourselves before doing what we know would please God. What a humbling thought!

Let us pray that God will help us to honestly open our hearts to Him. Let's ask for courage to see what's really there, so that He can cleanse us, search our minds, try our hearts and bless us with the good fruit of our doings.

"Behold, You desire truth in the innermost being, and in the hidden part You will make me know wisdom." (Psalm 51:6, NASB)

"Create in me a clean heart, O God; and renew a right spirit within me." (Psalm 51:10, KJV)

"You will seek me and find me when you seek me with all your heart." (Jeremiah 29:13, NIV)

Spiritual Fitness Involves Weight Training

"Wherefore seeing we also are compassed about with so great a cloud of witnesses, let us lay aside every weight, and the sin which doth so easily beset us, and let us run with patience the race that is set before us." (Hebrews 12:1, KJV)

If you're like millions of Americans, one of your top New Year's resolutions will be to get in better physical shape. While physical fitness is important, as the "body" of Christ, we should be more concerned with our spiritual fitness.

Interestingly, one of the main components of physical fitness – weight training—is also one of the main components of spiritual fitness. Hebrews 12:1 warns us to *"...lay aside every weight, and the sin which doth so easily beset us..."* The word "weight" in this scripture means "a burden or hindrance."

The Bible makes an important distinction between "weights" and "sins." Why the distinction? Because weights (burdens or hindrances) may not necessarily be sinful. But they are harmful to our spiritual progress.

What are some of the weights we need to lay aside?

♦ **Bad Habits.** These are your "issues." And while they may not seem so bad at first glance, they don't spiritually edify you or anyone else. Plus, as long as you keep up these bad habits, you remain wracked with guilt and unable to reach your full potential in Christ. These habits serve as the weapon of choice that the devil uses to keep you spiritually stagnant. If some of them were listed here, you might be tempted to compare them to others. However, because the Holy Spirit wants us to be free to serve Him, He will identify yours specifically if you will ask Him to show you (see Psalm 19:12).

♦ *Relationships.* These are unhealthy, dysfunctional friendships, alliances, romances or family relationships. Often there is an element of co-dependency. There may sometimes be physical, verbal, emotional or sexual abuse involved. Or there could simply be an unhealthy dependence on the emotional comfort a person provides that only the Lord should be providing. The Lord refers to these relationships as idolatry. Anytime you give someone a place of influence that only God should have, you become guilty of idol worship. Jeremiah 2:13 explains it this way: *"For my people have committed two evils; they have forsaken Me, the fountain of living waters, and hewed them out cisterns [ancient water bottles] broken cisterns, that can hold no water."*

In other words, God is saying, "I can supply all your needs, yet you choose to seek fulfillment in someone who can't compare to Me." Ask the Lord to reveal relationships that need to be either restructured or cut off entirely so that you can reach your full potential of spiritual and emotional freedom in Him. This process may cause temporary discomfort, but your freedom is worth the struggle! (See

Chapter Four: The Preparation of a Princess

Galatians 5:1)

◆ **Worry.** There will always be circumstances in our lives that cause us concern. Jesus said *"you will have troubles"* (John 16:33). If there is something we can do to affect a positive outcome—assuming we believe our actions to be in line with God's will—then we should by all means do it. But when we allow things that we have no control over to cause us mental and physical unrest, then our worry becomes a weight. The Bible commands us to give our concerns to God in prayer. *"Cast all your anxiety on him because he cares for you."* (1 Peter 5:7, NIV). We were never intended to carry the weight of worry alone. *"Then Jesus said, 'Come to me, all of you who are weary and carry heavy burdens, and I will give you rest.'"* (Matthew 11:28, NLT)

◆ **The Past.** Each of us has sinned and come short of God's glory, according to Romans 3:23. The greatest gift God could give us is the forgiveness that Jesus has already provided through His death on the cross. 1 John 1:9 says that *"if we confess our sins, God is faithful to forgive us and to cleanse us from all unrighteousness."* Yet, we often treat this precious promise as if it's simply not enough. Just like the woman who could not lift herself (see Luke 13:11-13) we go around bowed down with guilt and shame because of sins we committed years ago! Jesus says to you, "Woman, thou art loosed!" Why do you remain bound by that which Jesus has already freed? How long do you feel you need to pay for your sin? The answer is never! You can't do it because Christ already paid for it. Now, immediately walk in the freedom that Christ has given you through His precious blood that was shed just for you! *"Then neither do I condemn you," Jesus declared. "Go now and leave your life of sin."* (John 8:11b, NIV)

When we lay aside every weight and sins of our past, we find that we are free to be all that God wants us to be. We are free to accept His gift of salvation and to share that gift with others who need to experience the same freedom we have in Christ.

"*She girds herself with strength, and strengthens her arms.*" (Proverbs 31:17, NKJV)

"*Have not I commanded thee? Be strong and of a good courage; be not afraid, neither be thou dismayed: for the LORD thy God is with thee whithersoever thou goest.*" (Joshua 1:9, KJV)

"*Finally, my brethren, be strong in the Lord, and in the power of his might.*" (Ephesians 6:10, KJV)

Spiritual Fitness Involves "Wait" Training

Today's technology is designed to make life simpler, faster, and more convenient. The less time we have to wait to get what we want, the better, right? However, this is not always the case when it comes to our spiritual growth.

Just like physical makeovers, spiritual makeovers are not instant. They require an extensive process of careful evaluation, surgery, and an often painful period of healing and rehabilitation. We've seen how we need to become spiritually fit through intensive weight training. However, there is another important aspect to spiritual fitness: "wait" training. We need to learn to wait on the Lord in order to become stronger in our faith.

Waiting is never easy, but it has its benefits. Isaiah 40:31 says "*But they that wait upon the LORD shall renew their strength; they shall mount up with wings as eagles; they shall run, and not be weary; and they shall walk, and not faint.*" (KJV)

This particular scripture illustrates the benefits of waiting on God:

- ♦ **We will become stronger as we wait.** ("They that wait on the Lord shall renew their strength.")

- ♦ **We will develop the ability to see things from a heavenly perspective.** ("...they shall mount up with wings as eagles...")

Chapter Four: The Preparation of a Princess

❖ *We will remain energized while God takes us quickly through difficult situations.* *("...they shall run and not be weary...")*

❖ *We will be able to patiently endure when God chooses not to deliver us instantly from trouble.* *("...and they shall walk and not faint.")*

But what about those times when it seems we've waited "forever" and God still doesn't answer our prayers as we expect? It may be because He has decided that we're not ready to receive His answer or blessing. Isaiah 30:18 says, *"And therefore will the LORD wait, that he may be gracious unto you, and therefore will he be exalted, that he may have mercy upon you: for the LORD is a God of judgment: blessed are all they that wait for him."* (KJV)

In other words, there are times in our lives when, to quote a famous movie, we "can't handle the truth." So God waits until we're ready spiritually to receive the blessing, the answer or to learn the lesson.

There are other times when He withholds our request because He knows that if He gave us what we asked for, we would be destroyed. .In other words, He loves us enough to say "no" when necessary. *"The LORD will withhold no good thing from those who do what is right."* *(Psalm 84:11b, NLT)*

We are the daughters of a loving, compassionate King. If God withholds from us what we considered to be a blessing, we can trust that it is because we did not need it.

Whether we are required to wait on God or He waits on us, we become better spiritually prepared for whatever He has in store for us.

"Wait on the LORD: be of good courage, and he shall strengthen your heart: wait, I say, on the LORD." *(Psalm 27:14, AKJV)*

"The LORD is good unto them that wait for him, to the soul that seeketh him. It is good that a man should both hope and quietly

wait for the salvation of the LORD." (Lamentations 3:25-26, KJV)

"My soul, wait thou only upon God; for my expectation is from him." (Psalm 62:5, KJV)

A Mind is a Terrible Thing to Waste

Our minds, the center of our thoughts, have such a tremendous influence on every aspect of our lives. Our bodies are divinely programmed to act only upon impulse from our brains. We accomplish nothing without first imagining it.

Author Remez Sasson writes, "Imagination is the ability to form a mental image of something that is not perceived through the five senses. It is the ability of the mind to build mental scenes, objects or events that do not exist, are not present, or have happened in the past." It is a powerful tool that God gave to humans and includes the ability to think, to create, and to reason.

The mind is meant to absorb information, transform it into knowledge and lead it into action. Action and speech determine the quality of our lives and these come from the mind itself.

It has been said:
Watch your thoughts, they become words;
Watch your words, they become actions;
Watch your actions, they become habits;
Watch your habits, they become character;
Watch your character, for it becomes your destiny.

It is very important that we learn to control our thoughts. Though this may seem to be difficult, it is entirely possible and critical that we do so.

While we don't have total control over the types of information that are presented or introduced to us, we can control what we allow to remain in our minds. God's word gives us clear guidelines on what is acceptable to cultivate in our minds.

"Finally, brothers and sisters, whatever is true, whatever is noble, whatever is right, whatever is pure, whatever is lovely, what-

CHAPTER FOUR: THE PREPARATION OF A PRINCESS

ever is admirable—if anything is excellent or praiseworthy—think about such things." (Philippians 4:8, NIV)

The devil would love for us to fill our minds with fearful, lustful, angry, obsessive thoughts. But if we allow those kinds of thoughts to take up residence, our minds will become tainted and we will become guilty of "stinkin' thinkin'."

Jesus said, *"But the things that come out of a person's mouth come from the heart, and these defile them. For out of the heart come evil thoughts—murder, adultery, sexual immorality, theft, false testimony, slander. These are what defile a person..." (Matthew 15:18-20a, NIV)*

Society offers us plenty of opportunities to marinate our minds in things that do not please God. For example, there is no shortage of TV shows or films that condone adultery, sexual immorality, and celebrate cruelty to others to name a few. But God does not want us to imitate the world. Remember, a princess is no ordinary woman. Our standard is so much higher. *"Don't copy the behavior and customs of this world, but let God transform you into a new person by changing the way you think. Then you will learn to know God's will*

for you, which is good and pleasing and perfect." (Romans 12:2, NLT)

It follows, then, that if we want to act like Christ, we must also think like Him. Renewed minds will result in higher living—a kingdom mindset. *"Let this mind be in you which was also in Christ Jesus." (Philippians 2:5, KJV)*

This is difficult for us because, our thoughts are not naturally God's thoughts (see Isaiah 55:8).

Having the mind of Christ clarifies any distorted thinking we may have. Otherwise, we are subject to our own "carnal" (natural) minds. And the carnal mind can't understand the spiritual mind (see Romans 8:6-7).

There are benefits to having the mind of Christ, *"in whom are hidden all the treasures of wisdom and knowledge" (Colossians 2:3, NIV).*

♦ **We will experience fulfillment and peace of mind.** Romans 8:6 tells us that *"to be spiritually minded is life and peace."*

♦ **We will experience increased intimacy with God.** Isaiah 1:18 says that God wants us to come and reason with Him. He wants us to know His will for our lives (see Hebrews 13:21).

♦ **We will begin to desire to live a life of obedience to Him.** The psalmist asked God to give him understanding in keeping His laws and walking in His commandments so that he might *"turn away...from looking at worthless things" (Psalm 119:33-37).* Having any mind other than Christ's causes us to live a life of disobedience, rebellion and emptiness.

Learning to replace the lies of Satan with God's truth is the key to having the mind of Christ and living a life that is pleasing to God.

"We use our powerful God-tools for smashing warped philosophies, tearing down barriers erected against the truth of God, fitting every loose thought and emotion and impulse into the structure of

CHAPTER FOUR: THE PREPARATION OF A PRINCESS

life shaped by Christ. Our tools are ready at hand for clearing the ground of every obstruction and building lives of obedience into maturity." (2 Corinthians 10:5, MSG)

God will honor you as you seek to align your thoughts with His. *"I the Lord search the heart and examine the mind, to reward a man according to his conduct, according to what his deeds deserve" (Jeremiah 17:10, NIV).*

Princess, ask the Lord to show you the lies you have been believing. Determine to replace these lies with God's truths, found in His word, so that your relationship with Him and others will be transformed.

When we invest in these areas of spiritual restoration, an extreme spiritual makeover will begin to occur. Like Esther, we will experience renewed minds, new strength, greater faith and will become even more prepared to embrace the unique calling for which the King has anointed His daughters.

"And who knows but that you have come to your royal position for such a time as this?" (Esther 4:14b, NIV)

Priceless Pearl

"Being confident of this, that he who began a good work in you will carry it on to completion until the day of Christ Jesus."
Philippians 1:6

Princess Proclamation

Dear Heavenly Father:
You are not satisfied simply with me belonging to You. You want to fully prepare me to accomplish Your great purposes.

Like Esther, I need you to prepare me for what You have in store. Lord, I need an extreme spiritual makeover, from the inside out. Beautify me in every area of my life.

Chapter Four: The Preparation of a Princess

Help me control what I see, say, and follow after. Help me to put aside habits and relationships which do me and others harm. Teach me patience. I realize the only way to develop patience is when I have to wait on You to answer my prayers.

I trust You to develop Your character in me so that I will be ready to serve at the precise moment You present an opportunity.

In Jesus' name. Amen.

5

The Purification of a Princess

> "It is God's will that you should be sanctified..."
> –1 Thessalonians 4:3a, NIV

> "But by His doing you are in Christ Jesus, who became to us wisdom from God, and righteousness and sanctification, and redemption."
> –1 Corinthians 1:30, NASB

*J*ust as Queen Esther experienced a process of preparation, there is another equally important process through which every true Daughter of the King must go. Whenever God anoints His daughters for a special purpose, we must also go through the process of purification or "sanctification" as it is called in the Bible.

Sanctification is the process of making or becoming holy, set apart, or consecrated. It is the process of advancing in holiness;

CHAPTER FIVE: THE PURIFICATION OF A PRINCESS

where we are progressively transformed by the Lord into His likeness.

Suppose you had a rare and beautiful set of china, passed down to you from your great-great-grandmother. This china has been used for the most special of occasions for as long as you can remember. One day, you decide to host a dinner party to which an honored, distinguished guest has been invited to attend. You don't want to use your everyday dishes, some of which are mismatched. Only your fine china will do. You select which pieces you want to use, carefully washing and drying them by hand to make sure they sparkle beautifully, for this occasion requires your best presentation.

"If you keep yourself pure, you will be a special utensil for honorable use. Your life will be clean, and you will be ready for the Master to use you for every good work." (2 Timothy 2:21, NLT)

Likewise, God has hand-selected you, Princess, for a very special purpose.

"But ye are a chosen generation, a royal priesthood, a holy nation, a peculiar people; that ye should show forth the praises of him who hath called you out of darkness into his marvelous light." (1 Peter 2:9, KJV)

Sanctification is not a one-time event, nor is it instantaneous, because it is not the work of God alone. Rather, it is a gradual and repeated purging of sin, mindsets, and other actions that are harmful or unproductive to our walk with Christ. As God, through the work of the Holy Spirit, begins to identify our issues, we must be actively involved in submitting to God's will, resisting sin, seeking holiness, and working to be more godly (see Galatians 5:22-23). God then uses us for greater and higher purposes as we are obedient and submit to Him.

"Sanctification means the impartation of the holy qualities of Jesus Christ to me. It is the gift of His patience, love, holiness, faith, purity, and godliness that is exhibited in and through every sanctified soul. Sanctification is not drawing from Jesus the power to be

holy—it is drawing from Jesus the very holiness that was exhibited in Him, and that He now exhibits in me." —Oswald Chambers

The Process of Purification

Scripture beautifully illustrates a three-step process of sanctification: disrobe, dismiss and devote.

"Hearken, O daughter, and consider, and incline thine ear; forget also thine own people and thy father's house; so shall the king greatly desire thy beauty; for He is thy Lord, and worship thou him." (Psalm 45:10-11, KJV)

Deuteronomy 21:10-13 provides some background for this verse. Here, God outlines instructions for Israelite soldiers preparing for war.

"When you go to war against your enemies and the Lord your God delivers them into your hands and you take captives, if you notice among the captives a beautiful woman and are attracted to her, you may take her as your wife. Bring her into your home and have her shave her head, trim her nails and put aside the clothes she was wearing when captured. After she has lived in your house and mourned her father and mother for a full month, then you may go to her and be her husband and she shall be your wife." (NIV)

When a soldier went to war, was successful in defeating the enemy, and saw a woman among the captives whom he desired as a wife, she was to follow the instructions given in verses 12 and 13, and then be joined unto him in marriage.

Let us consider this to be a symbolic example of the relationship between the Daughters of the King and Christ Jesus, our Lord. Our Savior did spiritual battle with the devil for our souls. He redeemed us from the hand of the enemy (Psalm 107:2). The Bible tells of how Christ defeated Satan and led captivity captive (Ephesians 4:8). Christ gained the victory over the powers of hell as he died, took the keys of hell from Satan, and rose again on the third day (Revelations 1:18).

Chapter Five: The Purification of a Princess

The woman whom the Israelite soldier chose was required to go home with him, shave her head, cut her nails, change her clothes, and be joined unto him. Likewise, having obtained the victory in war, Christ does indeed see a beautiful woman He desires and invites her into relationship with Him.

"For you are a holy people, who belong to the LORD your God. Of all the people on earth, the LORD your God has chosen you to be his own special treasure." (Deuteronomy 7:6, NLT)

Indeed, Christ has already chosen you, Princess, for Himself.

Notice the woman also had to do her part.

"And he that is to be cleansed shall wash his clothes and shave off all his hair, and wash himself in water that he may be clean even all his hair shall he shave off, and he shall wash his clothes... and he shall be clean." (Leviticus 14:8-9, KJV)

"Take the Levites from among the children of Israel and cleanse them. And thus shalt thou do unto them to cleanse them: sprinkle water of purifying upon them, and let them shave all their flesh, and let them wash their clothes, and so make themselves clean." (Numbers 8:6-7, KJV)

Although chosen for her beauty, this woman needed cleansing. Probably from a pagan nation, she needed purifying as she knew nothing of the ways of the Israelites who served a holy and righteous God. Shaving of the head and clipping of the nails symbolized cleanliness and adherence to God's laws, as this was the only acceptable method of presenting herself as clean to her husband.

In addition to her physical cleansing, her former clothing called the "raiment of her captivity" was to be removed (Deuteronomy 21:13). These clothes symbolized her former life. Similarly, the chosen women of God are to take the first step in the process of purification.

❖ Disrobe

"You were taught, with regard to your former way of life, to put *off your old self, which is being corrupted by its deceitful desires."* (Ephesians 4:22, NIV)

God wants us to put off the "raiment of [our] captivity." These are works of the flesh such as lying, covetousness, deceitfulness, fornication, lusts, adultery (see Galatians 5:19) and other sins we committed before we were set free from the bondage of sin. When we were slaves to sin, we engaged freely in it. Since Christ has gone to war for us and has chosen us, we are now to "change clothes" and to "clothe yourselves with tenderhearted mercy, kindness, humility, gentleness, and patience. Make allowance for each other's faults, and forgive anyone who offends you. Remember, the Lord forgave you, so you must forgive others. Above all, clothe yourselves with love, which binds us all together in perfect harmony." (Colossians 3:12b-14, NLT)

This leads us to the second step in the process of purification.

♦ *Dismiss*

Next, the chosen woman was to mourn her parents for an entire month. At first glance, this would seem to be an odd requirement. However, it shows us the need to be sorry for the sins we have committed against the Lord before we knew Him.

We must dismiss the former life and its attachments (see Hebrews 12:1-2). The remembrance of sin ought to cause us to be remorseful because of what it cost Jesus.

"For when ye were the servants of sin (in bondage), ye were free from righteousness. What fruit had ye then in those things of which ye are now ashamed? For the end of those things is death." (Romans 6:20-21, KJV)

"For the kind of sorrow God wants us to experience leads us away from sin and results in salvation." (2 Corinthians 7:10, NLT)

Psalms 51:17 says that *"a broken and contrite heart"* God will not despise. We need to have a godly sorrow about the wrong things in which we were involved before our commitment to the Lord Jesus.

CHAPTER FIVE: THE PURIFICATION OF A PRINCESS

We should not take pleasure in the thought of them. Sin grieves the Lord and quenches the Holy Spirit, and we need to have a holy perspective of it, so that we won't blatantly sin against Him (see Psalms 19:13).

Psalms 45:10 also says that this "daughter" was to "forget also thine own people and thy father's house." She is encouraged to do what Paul says in Philippians 3:13. *"Brethren, I count not myself to have apprehended; but this one thing I do; forgetting those things which are behind, and reaching forth unto those things which are before, I press toward the mark for the prize of the high calling of God in Jesus Christ." (NIV)*

Jesus said, *"No man, having put his hand to the plough, and looking back, is fit for the kingdom of God." (Luke 9:62, KJV)*

There is a great danger in looking back with longing at those things which we did before we were reconciled to Christ. Looking back says that we do not trust the Lord. This causes us to lose our peace, our focus and our confidence in God. That's why the Psalmist wrote, *"thou wilt keep him in perfect peace whose mind is stayed on thee, because he trusteth in thee." (Isaiah 26:3, KJV)*

Keeping our focus on the Lord and what He is doing in our lives gives us peace. When we focus on what we don't have, we become anxious (see Hebrews 13:5). We also run the risk of becoming spiritually stagnant and unable to receive the full blessing of God (see Genesis 19:15-26 and Luke 17:32-33).

Once the woman's season of cleansing and mourning was completed, the marriage to her new husband could be consummated. This is the third and final step in the process of purification.

♦ Devote

"Listen, O daughter, give attention and incline your ear: Forget your people and your father's house; then the King will desire your beauty. Because He is your Lord, bow down to Him." (Psalm 45:10-11, NASB)

Because of what Christ has done for us, we are to love Him as we would love no other. Bowing down in worship is the outward expression of devotion. As a matter of fact, "worship" is defined as *"profound dedication; to give up or appropriate to a particular pursuit; to worship."* (Random House) The Bible instructs us to "follow (pursue) after holiness, without which no man shall see God." (Hebrews 12:14) We are to be devoted to God as a result of His devotion to us, and we are to worship Him.

Let the Daughters of the King **disrobe** from their former works and put on righteousness. **Dismiss** the memories your sinful pasts by renewing your minds and having a proper focus. Finally, **devote** yourselves to the service of the Lord, be grateful, trust in Him, and worship Him.

Means of Sanctification

God has many ways of sanctifying us.

◆ **Forgiveness:** In the daily process of living, we sin. Whether we intentionally sin (sins of commission) or fail to do the right thing (sins of omission), we need cleansing and forgiveness. 1 John 1:9 tells us that through Christ's death, burial and resurrection, forgiveness has been provided for us. *"If we confess our sins, he is faithful and just and will forgive us our sins and purify us from all unrighteousness."* Simply confessing our wrongs to God causes Him to forgive us and to clean us for His use once again.

◆ **Obedience:** When we make mistakes and foolish decisions, although we may have asked for forgiveness, we can still find ourselves heading in the wrong direction. It is then that we simply need to obey God's word. David wrote, *"How can a young person stay on the path of purity? By living according to your word."* (Psalm 119:9, NIV).

◆ **Scripture Memorization:** The third way God brings about

CHAPTER FIVE: THE PURIFICATION OF A PRINCESS

sanctification is closely related to the second. If you do not know what God's word says, it will be difficult to obey it. David wrote, *"I have hidden your word in my heart that I might not sin against you." (Psalm 119:11, NIV)*. Intentional study and memorization of God's word is essential to living a sanctified life. God desires that we know His will, which is recorded in His word. The Holy Spirit will bring it to our remembrance at the very moment we need wisdom and direction if we will commit to spending quality time in His word.

◈ **Tests and Trials:** The fourth way God brings about sanctification is through tests and trials. *"Dear friends, do not be surprised at the fiery ordeal that has come on you to test you, as though something strange were happening to you. But rejoice inasmuch as you participate in the sufferings of Christ, so that you may be overjoyed when his glory is revealed." (1 Peter 4:12-13, NIV)*. God allows us to experience challenges to test our mettle—to prove what we are truly made of.

◈ ***A Flaming Sword:*** God sometimes encourages our sanctification by confronting us with the negative consequences of sin. He will make it very difficult for us to do wrong, especially when He knows it's an area of great personal weakness. When Adam and Eve sinned against God in the Garden of Eden by eating from the tree of the knowledge of good and evil, God placed a cherubim with a flaming sword to block the path back to the tree of life. God was intent on preventing His children from returning to the very thing which had almost destroyed them. He put an almost insurmountable barrier in front of them to prevent them from doing so. They would have to be willing to face death in order to disobey God again. He still does it today. God will put a "hedge of protection" around his daughters, so that people who mean us harm will suddenly be repelled (see Job 1:9-11). Relationships we pursued that were harmful to us will no longer be open to us (see Proverbs 21:1). When we are unaware of what is happening, this can be frustrating, confusing or even painful. But God loves you so much that He would rather see you temporarily hurt than permanently destroyed. Still, the choice to do the right thing is ours.

"See, I set before you today life and prosperity, death and destruction. For I command you today to love the Lord your God, to walk in obedience to him, and to keep his commands, decrees and laws; then you will live and increase, and the Lord your God will bless you in the land you are entering to possess. But if your heart turns away and you are not obedient, and if you are drawn away to bow down to other gods and worship them, I declare to you this day that you will certainly be destroyed. You will not live long in the land you are crossing the Jordan to enter and possess. This day I call the heavens and the earth as witnesses against you that I have set before you life and death, blessings and curses. Now choose life, so that you and your children may live and that you may love the Lord your God, listen to his voice, and hold fast to him. For the Lord is your life, and he will give you many years in the land he swore to give to your fathers, Abraham, Isaac and Jacob." (Deuteronomy 30:15-20, NIV)

"Endure hardship as discipline; God is treating you as his children. For what children are not disciplined by their father? If you are not disciplined—and everyone undergoes discipline—then you are not legitimate, not true sons and daughters at all." (Hebrews 12:7-8, NIV)

♦ **The Pruning Process:** Our King is also a Gardener. In John 15, Jesus provides an interesting word picture. He says, *"I am the true vine, and my Father is the gardener. He cuts off every branch in me that bears no fruit, while every branch that does bear fruit he prunes so that it will be even more fruitful."* (John 15:1-2, NIV)

Through the process of pruning, the Gardener removes certain plant parts that are not required, that are no longer effective, or that are of no use to the plant. This is done to supply additional energy for the development of flowers, fruits, and limbs that remain on the plant.

Though it may appear to be unattractive until new foliage grows, the Gardner knows that proper pruning enhances the beauty of almost any tree or shrub. Pruning is done for a number of reasons.

♦ ***To train the plant:*** *"Blessed is the one whom God corrects; so do not despise the discipline of the Almighty."* (Job 5:17, NIV)

♦ ***To maintain plant health:*** *"But blessed is the one who trusts in the LORD, whose confidence is in him. They will be like a tree planted by the water that sends out its roots by the stream. It does not fear when heat comes; its leaves are always green. It has no worries in a year of drought and never fails to bear fruit."* (Jeremiah 17:7-8, NIV)

♦ ***To improve the quality of flowers, fruit, foliage or stems:*** *"Let us not become weary in doing good, for at the proper time we will reap a harvest if we do not give up."* (Galatians 6:9, NIV)

♦ ***To restrict growth:*** *"All scripture is inspired by God and is useful to teach us what is true and to make us realize what is wrong in our lives. It corrects us when we are wrong and teaches us to do* *what is right." (2 Timothy 3:16, NLT)*

The Gardener knows that pruning will ensure the overall health, beauty and productivity of the branches. He will do whatever it takes to remove sin and anything that limits our fruitfulness.

Spiritual pruning can take many forms. It may be sickness, hardships, or loss of material possessions or relationships. Whatever the method of pruning God uses, we can be assured that He cares for us and wants us to be fruitful, productive and prosperous. He wants to free us from whatever drains our life and energy.

"No discipline seems pleasant at the time, but painful. Later on, however, it produces a harvest of righteousness and peace for those who have been trained by it." (Hebrews 12:11, NIV)

Our King uses affliction to make us more responsive to His Word. Sometimes, when we have a problem, a particular verse of scripture will seem to jump off the page. In adversity, the Word of God comes alive.

God prunes us simply because He loves us. As Hebrews 12:6 says, *"Because the Lord disciplines the one he loves, and he chastens everyone he accepts as his son" (NIV).* If we remember that God is trying to make us more fruitful, we can look past the pain of the pruning process to the goal: to be more like Christ.

A Palace Fit for a King

Joy to the world the Lord is come! Let earth receive her King! Let every heart prepare Him room...

Let every heart prepare Him room.

She agonized in labor—the sharp contractions racking her belly with excruciating pain—as her husband desperately sought shelter. At any moment, she would give birth to their first child.

There were no hospitals. No hotel rooms available. No one opened their home to give this desperate couple a dignified, private place to experience one of humanity's most sacred and intimate acts. Instead, Mary was forced to give birth in a filthy stable, surrounded by

CHAPTER FIVE: THE PURIFICATION OF A PRINCESS

barn animals, and laid her newborn son, Jesus, in a feeding trough.

Throughout His physical life on planet Earth, the One who created the earth and all that is in it had *"no place to lay his head."* (Luke 9:58). When Christ died, was buried and rose again, He promised His disciples that the Holy Spirit would reside in the hearts of those who received Him as Lord and Savior. Now, our hearts have become the permanent dwelling place of the Holy Spirit, yet still we must "prepare Him room."

"Don't you know that you yourselves are God's temple and that God's Spirit dwells in your midst?" (1 Corinthians 3:16, NIV)

Preparing room for the Holy Spirit involves our willingness to make Him comfortable and welcomed into every area of our lives.

Just as we would specially prepare our homes to receive an honored guest, we need to ensure that our hearts are clean, pure and made ready for the indwelling of the Holy Spirit. There should be no area of our lives which is "off limits" or closed off to the Holy Spirit; no area to which He cannot have full access.

Secret sins. Hidden habits. Our King insists on having access to even these places. He desires to know us intimately in every area of our lives. He wants to make our hearts His home, but He cannot and will not do so unless we welcome Him there.

"How can I know all the sins lurking in my heart? Cleanse me from these hidden faults." (Psalm 19:12, NLT)

"Search me, God, and know my heart; test me and know my anxious thoughts. See if there is any offensive way in me, and lead me in the way everlasting." (Psalm 139:23-24, NIV)

"Behold, thou desirest truth in the inward parts: and in the hidden part thou shalt make me to know wisdom." (Psalm 51:6, KJV)

Welcoming God means we willingly acknowledge that we belong to Him and that all we have is His.

"Or do you not know that your body is the temple of the Holy Spirit who is in you, whom you have from God, and you are not your own? For you were bought at a price; therefore glorify God

in your body and in your spirit, which are God's." (1 Corinthians 6:19-20, NKJV)

Preparing Him room means that we search our hearts, confessing our sins and courageously addressing any attitude or action that we know would displease Him.

When we open our hearts to the leading of the Holy Spirit, allowing Him to live the life of Christ through us, He makes us into a beautiful dwelling place—a palace fit for our King.

"For we are the temple of the living God, just as God said, 'I will live in them and will walk among them, and I will be their God, and they will be my people." (2 Corinthians 6:16b, NIV)

Chapter Five: The Purification of a Princess

Priceless Pearl

"Or do you not know that your body is the temple of the Holy Spirit who is in you, whom you have from God, and you are not your own? For you were bought at a price; therefore glorify God in your body and in your spirit, which are God's."
1 Corinthians 6:19-20

Princess Proclamation

Dear Heavenly Father:
I ask You to purify me and make me suitable for Your use. At times, this will require sacrifice on my part. I may be unable to do the things I used to do, or be in relationship with people who discourage me from following You.

At other times, I will simply need to surrender my will to Yours and trust that the changes You are making in my life will bring You glory.

Make me into a dwelling place You can enjoy so that I will experience the best life possible with You.

Thank you for choosing me to be Your temple here on earth.

In Jesus' name. Amen.

CHAPTER FIVE: THE PURIFICATION OF A PRINCESS

Lyrical Love Letter

FORGIVE ME

There's no one I can to turn to.
No place I can hide.
No more strength to fight against
The guilt I feel inside.
The accuser comes to steal away
The peace and joy I have.
And he's constantly reminding me
What I've done in my past.

How can You forgive me
After the wrong I've done?
Can You clear away the shame
That falls like rain
And hides away the sun?
How could You give your life for me,
O perfect Holy One?
I cannot comprehend.
And so I ask again
How can You forgive me?

Forgive me.
Forgive me.

Oh, if you confess with your mouth He is Lord
And believe in your heart that He lives,
You will be saved for the price has been paid.
Every sin, every fault He forgives.

That's how can You forgive me
After the wrong I've done.
The moment that I let You in
You took my sin
And laid it on Your Son.
And when He gave His life for me
The victory I won.

I'm covered by Your grace
Because You took my place.
No longer bound by shame
For I'm called by Your name.
That day at Calvary
Was when You set me free.

And it's when You forgave me.
Forgave me.
Forgave me.
So glad that You forgave me!

6

The Promises of a Princess

Now the Lord said to Abram, "Go from your country and your kindred and your father's house to the land that I will show you. And I will make of you a great nation, and I will bless you and make your name great, so that you will be a blessing. I will bless those who bless you, and him who dishonors you I will curse, and in you all the families of the earth shall be blessed."
–Genesis 12:1-3, ESV

So in Christ Jesus you are all children of God through faith, for all of you who were baptized into Christ have clothed yourselves with Christ. There is neither Jew nor Gentile, neither slave nor free, nor is there male and female, for you are all one in Christ Jesus. If you belong to Christ, then you are Abraham's seed, and heirs according to the promise. –Galatians 3:26-29, NIV

The lines have fallen for me in pleasant places; indeed, I have a beautiful inheritance. –Psalm 16:6, ESV

"The Spirit Himself testifies with our spirit that we are children of God, and if children, heirs also, heirs of God and fellow

heirs with Christ, if indeed we suffer with Him so that we may also be glorified with Him."
—Romans 8:16-17, NASB

"**And she lived happily ever after...**"

That's how we like fairy tales to end—happily. We live in a world so full of disappointments that every once in a while, we could all use a good dose of princes and princesses riding off into the sunset to live happily ever after.

One particular tale comes to mind and goes something like this:

A man becomes lost in the woods and stumbles upon a mysterious castle. The master of the house, the Beast, is infuriated by the man's intrusion on his property and holds him hostage. The man's daughter, Beauty, discovers her father's whereabouts and offers herself as a hostage in exchange for the release of her father. The Beast accepts this exchange, and Beauty remains hopelessly imprisoned by this

CHAPTER SIX: THE PROMISES OF A PRINCESS

horrendous creature. Although the Beast is hideous and emotionally cruel to Beauty, they somehow develop a deep friendship. Beauty's kindness softens the Beast's evil, hardened heart, and he eventually becomes the gorgeous prince he once was. They fall in love, marry and live happily ever after.

A television version of this story aired in the 1990s about a successful career woman who discovers the Beast, a monster-like creature who lives deep down in a sewer. Somehow, they begin a secret love affair, and her deepest desire is to leave all that she has accomplished—her career, her education, her family, her property—and be joined to the Beast in his lair.

Does this sound like a far cry from reality? Unfortunately, it happens all too often.

Perverted Promises

The enemy, whom the Bible calls the "Beast" (Revelation 13) can sometimes lull us into taking a spiritual "vacation." He will go to any limit to destroy your testimony and your life so that you cannot be a blessing to the world. The Beast's goal is to lure you in and to hold you hostage spiritually. He wants you to become so acclimated to his (sub) standard of living that you get spiritual "amnesia," forgetting who you are and where you came from.

Wake up, sister! Remember that you are a princess, a beautiful and priceless Daughter of the King! And the King will go to any limit to get you back. He purchased you and made you His. You belong to Him forever, and He will not allow you to live in filth, perversion, spiritual poverty, guilt, and fear. You were designed to be holy, sanctified, righteous, and wealthy, with a clear conscience in a life of freedom and faith! Please don't ever forget that!

"Christ has set us free to live a free life. So take your stand! Never again let anyone put a harness of slavery on you." (Galatians 5:1, MSG)

How does the Beast lure the princess into his kingdom? By causing you to fall for his perverted "promises" instead of the promises of God. Let me alert you to some of the promises and the lies of the Beast:

◆ ***"Follow me, and I can fulfill your desires quickly."***
The King says, *"Delight yourself in the LORD, and He will give you the desires of your heart. Commit your way to the LORD, Trust also in Him, and He will do it." (Psalm 37:4-5, NASB)*

◆ ***"Follow me and I will give you happiness, success, and prosperity apart from God and His principles."***
The King says, *"There is a way which seemeth right unto a man, but the end thereof are the ways of death." (Proverbs 14:12, KJV)*

"...and as long as [you] seek the Lord, God will make [you] to prosper." (2 Chronicles 26:5)

"Trust in the LORD with all thine heart; and lean not unto thine own understanding. In all thy ways acknowledge him, and he shall direct thy paths." (Proverbs 3:5-6, KJV)

◆ ***"Follow me and you can have your cake and eat it too."***
The King says, *"Choose you this day whom you will serve..." (Joshua 24:15)*

"I know your deeds, that you are neither cold nor hot. I wish you were either one or the other! So, because you are lukewarm—neither hot nor cold—I am about to spit you out of my mouth." (Revelation 3:16, NIV)

"A double-minded man is unstable in all his ways." (James 1:8, KJV)

◆ ***"God doesn't care about you."***
The King says, *"Cast all your care upon [Me] for I care for you." (1 Peter 5:7)*

"Look at the birds of the air; they do not sow or reap or store away in barns, and yet your heavenly Father feeds them. Are you

CHAPTER SIX: THE PROMISES OF A PRINCESS

not much more valuable than they?"(Matthew 6:26, NIV)

"The LORD appeared to us in the past, saying: 'I have loved you with an everlasting love; I have drawn you with unfailing kindness.'" (Jeremiah 31:3, NIV)

💎 **"You have sinned too much to be forgiven."**

The King says, *"If [you] confess [your] sins, [I] am faithful and just to forgive [you] and to cleanse [you] from all unrighteousness."* (1 John 1:9)

"...And Jesus said unto her, neither do I condemn you; go, and sin no more." (John 8:11, NKJV)

💎 **"No one understands or cares about what you are going through."**

The King says, *"Be anxious for nothing, but in everything, by prayer and supplication with thanksgiving let your requests be made known to God. And the peace of God, which surpasses all comprehension, will guard your hearts and minds in Christ Jesus."* (Philippians 4:6-7, NASB)

"You know when I sit down and when I rise up [my entire life, everything I do]; You understand my thoughts from afar." (Psalm 139:2, AMP)

Princess, you must commit to searching the scripture and memorizing God's word so that you can recall God's many promises to you. The word of God is full of them. In the Appendix, you will find "The Royal Decree." It is a list of some of the promises of God. This should encourage you to look for more on your own.

The choice is yours to believe God's promises to you.

"I rejoice in your word like one who discovers a great treasure." (Psalm 119:162, NLT)

"Your laws are my treasure; they are my heart's delight." (Psalm 119:111, NLT)

Please don't allow the Beast to convince you that you are not worthy of God's blessing and God's best. We have been made righteous in Christ. Keep a Princess' Perspective and trust your Father, the King, to do what He said He could and would do for you.

He loves you and His word never fails!

CHAPTER SIX: THE PROMISES OF A PRINCESS

Priceless Pearl

"For no matter how many promises God has made, they are 'Yes' in Christ. And so through him the 'Amen' is spoken by us to the glory of God."
2 Corinthians 1:20

Princess Proclamation

God's promises to me are amazing.

I can claim every one because I am God's child. His power is unlimited. His riches in glory are immeasurable. God's plans for me go beyond what I can ask or even think to ask of Him.

I trust God, by faith, to do all that He said He would do.

God gives me wisdom to search His word to discover those

promises, so that I will remain encouraged when I don't see anything happening.

I have a beautiful inheritance coming to me simply because I am the King's daughter.

I am blessed beyond measure.

Chapter Six: The Promises of a Princess

Lyrical Love Letter

DAUGHTER OF THE KING

I am a Princess, a daughter of the King.
Let me tell you all about the day it came to be.
One day I heard that the King was issuing a royal decree.
It said that anyone who would receive His Son
Could be a part of His royal family.
Now I'm a Princess, a daughter of the King.

I am a Princess, a daughter of the King.
But this is not a fairy tale, it's real as real can be.
He clothed me in purple, gave me a crown of life
And He made me royalty.
That's why I bow my knees and why I lift my hands.
I give Him praise for all He's done for me.
For I'm a Princess, a daughter of the King.

Dressed in His righteousness, filled with His holiness,
Seated in the heavenlies, that's what He did for me.
Forever I will reign, never to die again.
I am a Princess, a daughter of the King.

S. Kristi Douglas

I am a Princess, a daughter of the King.
I gave my heart and in exchange what wealth He gave to me!
And did you know the King's still issuing His royal decree?
It says that anyone who will receive His Son
Can be a part of this royal family and be
A son or a daughter of the King.

Dressed in His righteousness, filled with His holiness,
Seated in the heavenlies, that's what He did for me.
Forever I will reign, never to die again.
I am a Princess, a daughter of the King.

He made the sacrifice and gave me a crown of life.
He gave me joy untold, I'll walk the streets of gold.
Someday my Prince will come, He is the Holy One.
That's why I bow my knees and why I lift my hands.
I am a Princess, a daughter of the King of Kings.
I am a Princess, a daughter of the King.

Oh, worship the King!

7

The Power of a Princess

> "Every battle is won before it is fought."
> —Sun Tzu

> "Whether you realize it or not, you are part of an epic battle. And God does not want His daughters unarmed or caught unaware."
> —Lisa Bevere

> "For though we walk in the flesh, we do not war according to the flesh. For the weapons of our warfare are not of the flesh, but mighty before God to the casting down of strongholds. Casting down imaginations, and every high thing that is exalted against the knowledge of God, and bringing every thought into captivity to the obedience of Christ."
> —2 Corinthians 10:3-5, ASV

God's people were in the fight of their lives.

Twenty years was a long time to be oppressed. Because of their disobedience, God allowed the children of Israel to be enslaved under the cruel rule of King Jabin and his commander, the sadistic Sisera.

Now, God heard their cries for deliverance and promised Deborah, their judge and advisor, that He would finally defeat their enemies in battle. Sure enough, God honored His word and all of Sisera's soldiers were wiped out by the Israelite army. However, Sisera himself managed to escape.

He fled to the tent of a simple countrywoman named Jael, whose husband was his ally. Surely, underneath this nondescript canvas shelter he could find a safe place to rest until he could figure out his next move. Yes, he would ask for a cool drink, nap for a bit...maybe just clear his head.

Little did he know that Jael would do it for him.

When Sisera entered Jael's tent, she welcomed him, offering him a comfortable place to lie down. She gave him a warm, soothing cup of milk and covered him with a blanket. As soon as he fell asleep, she moved in for the kill.

"Then Jael, Heber's wife, took a tent-pin, and took a hammer in her hand, and went softly unto him, and smote the pin into his temples, and it pierced through into the ground; for he was in a deep sleep; so he swooned and died." (Judges 4:21, ASV)

The grisly story of Sisera's demise at the hand of Jael is told in Judges 4. God used this powerful princess to fulfill His promise to His people, that He would *"deliver (Sisera) into thy hand."* (Judges 4:7). Jael's "she-roism" literally placed the final nail in the coffin of God's enemy and allowed God's people to enjoy 40 years of freedom from bondage.

"We wrestle not against flesh and blood..." (Ephesians 6:12).

Let's face it. War is not pretty. Warriors must be brave, strong, and believe with all their hearts that the cause for which they are fighting is worth risking their very lives. Although it is unpleasant and even frightening, God requires that His daughters know how to do battle with the enemy.

Jael was successful in annihilating Sisera because she understood four important principles that we, too, must grasp if we will become the powerful princess warriors God has called us to be.

Powerful princesses know how to:

💎 **I.D. the Enemy:** Over the years, Jael had heard and perhaps even witnessed the cruel treatment of the children of Israel. Through her husband, Heber, she had kinship ties with God's people. However, her husband had an alliance with King Jabin, Israel's enemy. Jael must have felt some sympathy for and loyalty to the Israelites because she identified Sisera as their enemy and was moved to action because of their plight.

We, too, have an enemy—the devil—who *"prowls around like a roaring lion looking for someone to devour." (1 Peter 5:8, NIV)* We are urged to stay alert and be on the lookout for him. Our adversary and his host of demons have a single, driving purpose: obliterate the children of God. Satan lives to accuse us of wrong doing (see Revelation 12:10). He seeks opportunities to discourage and defeat us. He has come to "steal and kill and destroy" the blessing and joy that God intends for us (see John 10:10). Like Sisera, the devil's desire is to oppress us for our entire lives, so that we will not accomplish the divine purpose God has planned for us. We must identify who he is so that we will know how to stop him in his tracks.

💎 **Prevent the Enemy from Advancing:** Jael realized that the only way to stop Sisera from rising again was to kill him and she seized her opportunity. She identified his weaknesses (he was tired and hungry) and took advantage of his weakened state.

Likewise, the word of God says that we need *"to keep Satan from taking advantage of us; for we are not ignorant of his schemes." (2 Corinthians 2:11, AMP)*

We must be careful and purposeful when engaging in spiritual warfare with the devil. We cannot take his attacks lightly but must be intentional and aggressive in doing whatever it takes to stop him.

"*Submit yourselves then to God. Resist the devil and he will flee from you*" *(James 4:7, NIV).* The word "resist" in this passage is a Greek military term meaning to strongly resist an opponent or refuse to be move backward. The word "flee" suggests one who is escaping or running away.

Satan is a relentless opponent who will not stop advancing until we issue a fatal blow using the powerful spiritual weapons that God has provided.

◆ **Use Weapons of Mass Destruction:** During Jael's lifetime, tent making was "woman's work" and the women became experts in all phases of pitching and striking tents. For this reason, Jael was highly skilled in the use of a hammer and tent pin and used what was readily available to serve as her weapon of choice.

"*Therefore put on the full armor of God, so that when the day of evil comes, you may be able to stand your ground, and after you have done everything, to stand.*" *(Ephesians 6:13, NIV).*

God has given us powerful spiritual weapons which are outlined in Ephesians 6. The Bible calls this the "full armor" of God and instructs us to always be dressed and ready for war so that we can withstand our enemy's onslaughts.

"*Stand firm then, with the **belt of truth** buckled around your waist, with the **breastplate of righteousness** in place, and with your **feet fitted with the readiness that comes from the gospel of peace**. In addition to all this, take up the **shield of faith**, with which you can extinguish all the flaming arrows of the evil one. Take the **helmet of salvation** and the **sword of the Spirit**, which is the word of God. And **pray** in the Spirit on all occasions with all kinds of prayers and requests. With this in mind, be alert and **always keep on praying** for all the Lord's people.*" *(Ephe-*

sians 6:14-18, NIV)

Our armor is designed to protect us during spiritual battles.

The **belt of truth** keeps us secure in Christ and makes all the other pieces of armor effective. The belt of truth holds our armor in place. It helps us to remain grounded in what the word of God says about every situation (the truth about you from the King's point of view). Jesus said, *"If you hold to my teaching, you are really my disciples. Then you will know the truth, and the truth will set you free." (John 8:31b-32, NIV)*

The **breastplate of righteousness** represents the righteousness of Christ, which covers and protects us. *"God made him who had no sin to be sin for us, so that in him we might become the righteousness of God" (2 Corinthians 5:21, NIV).* It is only because of the righteousness of Christ that we are acceptable to God. When we rely on our own goodness, we will repeatedly fall short because we cannot compare to Christ's holiness (Romans 3:23 and Isaiah 64:6). One of Satan's most effective attacks is to tempt us to believe that our acceptance by

God is based on our performance for him. Once we believe that lie, it easy for Satan to distract us from the key to our spiritual lives—that we are accepted and adored by God not because of what we do for him, but solely because of what Jesus has already done for us. This is the gift of grace.

"'No weapon formed against you will succeed, and you will refute any accusation raised against you in court. This is the heritage of the LORD's servants, and their righteousness is from Me.' This is the LORD's declaration." (Isaiah 54:17, HCSB)

The **shoes of the readiness of the gospel of peace** represent the stability and protection that come from having a heart guarded by God's peace. Shoes allow us to move without restriction or fear as we turn our full attention to the battle at hand. Our shoes move us onward to proclaim true peace, which is made available to us only in Christ. *"Do not be anxious about anything, but in every situation, by prayer and petition, with thanksgiving, present your requests to God. And the peace of God, which transcends all understanding, will guard your hearts and your minds in Christ Jesus."* (Philippians 4:6-7, NIV).

The **shield of faith** allows us to defend ourselves from the lies of the enemy by recalling and affirming the promises of God. Although the devil is expert at hurling darts of fear, doubt and worry in our direction, the only time they can hit us is when we lower our shield of faith—when we stop believing that God is in control and that He is working everything out for our good. The shield exists to "extinguish all the flaming arrows of the evil one," allowing us to do battle with confidence, knowing we are protected. *"Who through faith are shielded by God's power until the coming of the salvation that is ready to be revealed in the last time."* (1 Peter 1:5, NIV)

The **helmet of salvation** provides us with assurance of our eternal security in Christ. The enemy wants to make us doubt our salvation. Once we have received the gift of salvation through faith in Christ, God promises that we belong to Him forever. There is nothing we or the devil can do to change that. Jesus said, *"My sheep listen to my voice; I know them, and they follow me. I give them eternal life, and they shall never perish; no one will snatch them out of my hand. My Father, who has given them to me, is greater than all; no one can snatch them out of my Father's hand. I and the Father are one." (John 10:27-30, NIV)*

The helmet protects our minds from doubting the truth of God's saving work for us. *"Since we belong to the day, we must be serious and put the armor of faith and love on our chests, and put on a helmet of the hope of salvation"* (1 Thessalonians 5:8, HCSB). In Jesus Christ our souls are eternally secure.

The **sword of the spirit** is the word of God, which does not change (see Numbers 23:19). This is our only offensive weapon—the only one we need—and it is the means by which we can slice into the enemy's logic and lies when we wield it skillfully. As princess warriors, we must use the word of God to discern the truth and then obey it. When God's Word shows us the error of our ways, we can use this spiritual weapon to "surgically" remove offensive thoughts and actions.

"For the word of God is alive and active. Sharper than any double-edged sword, it penetrates even to dividing soul and spirit, joints and marrow; it judges the thoughts and attitudes of the heart." (Hebrews 4:12, NIV)

If Christ used the word of God to counter Satan's attacks (see Matthew 4:4, 7, 10), how much more must the Daughters of the King follow His example and learn to live "by every word that proceeds from the mouth of God!"

Our Secret Weapon

Finally, there is a secret weapon which God has given us to fight enemy forces. The enemy does not have access to it. He cannot stop it. The devil has no defense for this type of weapon.

It is prayer.

To some extent, the effectiveness of the other weapons relies on our skillfulness and consistency of use. But prayer is the equivalent of dropping a GPS-guided missile (God Positioned System) directly on our circumstances.

"Prayer is warfare activity. A prayer closet should be a foxhole with sandbags and bullet shells. We are at war! Prayer is not chatting on the phone with God. It is the frantic radio calls of a platoon under heavy fire calling for air support. God! Send in help! We need your intervention, and we need it now, or we are not going to survive!" —J.D. Myers

God's power is unlimited. His response to our prayers is constrained only by His perfect will and our faith. Through Christ, we have direct access to our heavenly power source. By God's power, we can do the miraculous!

"The effectual fervent prayer of a righteous man availeth much. Elias was a man subject to like passions as we are, and he prayed earnestly that it might not rain: and it rained not on the earth by the space of three years and six months. And he prayed again, and the heaven gave rain, and the earth brought forth her fruit." (James 5:16b-18, KJV)

Worth Fighting For

With the freedom of the Israelites at stake, Jael decided that her personal risk of harm was minor in comparison to what could be gained if she was successful in executing her plan. We fight against a much more fearsome opponent who, unlike Sisera, is alert, heavily armed and ready for battle. If we are not careful, we can easily forget about the severity of this battle. But make no mistake—our spiritual lives and future in God's kingdom are on the line. If we lose this war, we lose everything.

Though we need to be alert, we need never be fearful. Just as God was on the side of His children, God is on your side. Just as He promised the Israelites victory, He has already promised victory for the Daughters of the King.

"I have told you these things, so that in me you may have peace. In this world you will have trouble. But take heart! I have overcome the world." *(John 16:33, NIV)*

"For everyone born of God overcomes the world. This is the victory that has overcome the world, even our faith." *(1 John 5:4, NIV)*

"The weapons we fight with are not the weapons of the world. On the contrary, they have divine power to demolish strongholds."
2 Corinthians 10:4

I am in the fight of my life.
I have an enemy whose mission is to hunt, kill and destroy me.
However, I have a Father whose mission is to protect and prosper me despite the weapons formed against me.
He says the weapons the enemy directs at me will fail.
If I use the weapons provided by my Father, I am sure to win.

Chapter Seven: The Power of a Princess

I have been given power to overcome every obstacle. Greater is He who is in me than He who is in the world.

I am fearless.

I am an overcomer.

I am victorious.

THIS BATTLE

A battle cry arises. A war is fought within
Between the me I long to be and who I've always been.
Refusing to surrender; resolving to obey.
I sound the trumpet of my prayers and hear my Captain say,

"I'll fight this battle.
I'll fight this battle.
I'll never give you
What you can't handle.
Faith is the victory
And it's all worth fighting for.
I'll fight this battle
For I've already won the war."

And though the combat rages and many soldiers fall;
Amid the noise the Captain's voice rings clearly through it all.
And though enemies are ruthless and wounded I may be,
Upheld by grace His strong embrace brings healing back to me.

"I'll fight this battle.

Chapter Seven: The Power of a Princess

I'll fight this battle.
I'll never give you
What you can't handle.
Faith is the victory
And it's all worth fighting for.
I'll fight this battle
For I've already won the war."

"Stand still and see your salvation lies in Me.
No, you will not need to fight.
All that's wrong I will make right.
I know you're tired of going 'round and 'round.
So just shout and see these walls come tumbling down!"

"I'll fight this battle.
I'll fight this battle.
I'll never give you
More than you can handle.
You'll win fighting on your knees;
Singing praises ever more.
Let Me fight this battle.
Have no fear at all.
For I will fight this battle.
I've already won the war.
Oh, we've won for sure!

8

The Prayers of a Princess

"Prayer is not asking. Prayer is putting oneself in the hands of God, at His disposition, and listening to His voice in the depths of our hearts."
—Mother Theresa

"Pray without ceasing."
—1 Thessalonians 5:17, KJV

The Purpose of Prayer

The perfect example of obedience in prayer was Christ himself. Although His days were packed with great pressures and responsibilities, He always made time for prayer. It was His top priority. He understood the need to regroup, relax, relate and release through the act of prayer. Now if the Son of God was so dependent upon His fellowship in prayer alone with His Father, how much more should the Daughters of the King spend time alone in His presence!

Many, in an effort to appear to be spiritual, have made prayer much more complicated than it needs to be. Indeed, prayer is a spiritual and sacred event. It is the means by which we enter into the very presence of our holy and righteous heavenly father. But the process of prayer is actually quite simple.

Prayer is simply having a conversation with God. Prayer involves talking and listening. We speak to God and in turn, He speaks to us. Like any relationship, this two-way exchange allows us to get to know God intimately and is the means through which we engage Him on our behalf regarding our needs, desires, and feelings.

The Process of Prayer

The process of prayer can be summarized through the acronym A.C.T.S:

💎 *"A" is for "Adoration."* This is where we offer our praise to God, expressing our love and worship simply for who He is. *"I love You, O LORD, my strength" (Psalm 18:1). "Come, let us worship and bow down, Let us kneel before the LORD our Maker" (Psalm 95:6, KJV).*

💎 *"C" is for "Confession."* This is where we confess to God our sins of commission (what we've done) as well as sins of omission (what we've failed to do). Confession is what keeps the lines of communication between God and us clear and open. *"If I regard iniquity in my heart, the Lord will not hear me" (Psalm 66:18, KJV). "If we confess our sins, he is faithful and just and will forgive us our sins and purify us from all unrighteousness" (1 John 1:9, NIV).*

◈ **"T" is for "Thanksgiving."** This is where we thank God, expressing gratitude for the great things He has done in and for us. *"O give thanks unto the Lord; for he is good: for his mercy endureth forever." (Psalm 136:1, KJV)*

◈ **"S" is for "Supplication."** This is where we implore God passionately to act on our behalf or to meet the needs of others. *"Do not be anxious about anything, but in every situation, by prayer and petition, with thanksgiving, present your requests to God. And the peace of God, which transcends all understanding, will guard your hearts and your minds in Christ Jesus." (Philippians 4:6-7, NIV)*

A Picture of Prayer

In Luke chapter 11, at the request of one of His disciples, Jesus teaches a lesson on how to pray. After demonstrating a pattern for prayer (commonly known as "The Lord's Prayer"), He tells a story.

"Then Jesus said to them, 'Suppose you have a friend, and you go to him at midnight and say, "Friend, lend me three loaves of bread; a friend of mine on a journey has come to me, and I have no food to offer him." And suppose the one inside answers, "Don't bother me. The door is already locked, and my children and I are in bed. I can't get up and give you anything." I tell you, even though he will not get up and give you the bread because of friendship, yet because of your shameless audacity he will surely get up and give you as much as you need.

So I say to you: Ask and it will be given to you; seek and you will find; knock and the door will be opened to you. For everyone who asks receives; the one who seeks finds; and to the one who knocks, the door will be opened.

Which of you fathers, if your son asks for a fish, will give him a snake instead? Or if he asks for an egg, will give him a scorpion? If you then, though you are evil, know how to give good gifts to your

Chapter Eight: The Prayers of a Princess

children, how much more will your Father in heaven give the Holy Spirit to those who ask him!" (Luke 11:5-13, NIV)

Jesus' illustration shows us that effective prayer must be:

💎 **Persistent:** *"I tell you, even though he will not get up and give you the bread because of friendship, yet because of your shameless audacity, he will surely get up..." (Luke 11:8, NIV)*

When a need is identified, you must go to God with your unrelenting requests until the need is met. This quality of persistence was displayed in many great men and women of faith throughout the Bible. Jacob wrestled an angel all night long for a blessing, crying *"I won't let go unless you bless me" (Genesis 32:22-31)*. We are encouraged to pray continuously, without becoming disheartened by the amount of time it may take God to answer. Our faith will be rewarded only if we do not give up (see Galatians 6:9).

💎 **Purposeful:** *"Friend, lend me three loaves of bread; a friend of mine on a journey has come to me, and I have no food to offer him." (Luke 11:5b-6, NIV)*

Our prayers should be uttered with specificity. We must come to God with clear, precise requests. Although He already knows what we need before we ask Him, we must tell God what we need and why (see Matthew 6:8). This causes us to have complete assurance that God answers our specific prayers. *"When you ask, you do not receive, because you ask with wrong motives, that you may spend what you get on your pleasures." (James 4:3, NIV)*

💎 **Persuasive:** *"...he will surely get up and give you as much as you need. So I say to you: Ask and it will be given to you; seek and you will find; knock and the door will be opened to you." (Luke 11:8b-9, NIV)*

💎 **Powerful:** Because of the persistence and purposefulness of our passionate requests, we will be able to convince God to act on our behalf. *"For everyone who asks receives; the one who seeks* *finds; and to the one who knocks, the door will be opened." (Luke 11:10, NIV)*

"This is the confidence we have in approaching God: that if we ask anything according to his will, he hears us. And if we know that he hears us—whatever we ask—we know that we have what we asked of him." (1 John 5:14-15, NIV)

A Praying Princess

Simply review the stories of great women and men of God and you will begin to see a common thread. Each of them accomplished amazing things for God's glory once they learned to tap into the power of prayer.

The book of 1 Samuel chapters 1 and 2 tell the story of Hannah, a praying princess. During Hannah's lifetime, the ability to have children was equated with the favor and blessing of God. Unable to bear children, Hannah persistently prayed that God would open her womb.

To add insult to injury, her husband's second wife, Peninnah, who had borne several children, taunted her openly about her infertility. This only added to Hannah's immense heartache and shame, and she would grieve to the point of being unable to eat.

Her husband, who loved Hannah more than Peninnah, would try to appease his wife by showering her with gifts and his attention, but this only seemed to increase tension between the two women.

Year after year this dysfunctional cycle continued, until one day, the Bible says Hannah "stood up" (1 Samuel 1:9). Hannah prayed to the Lord as if something suddenly arose in her spirit proclaiming "enough is enough."

"In her deep anguish Hannah prayed to the Lord, weeping bitterly. And she made a vow, saying, 'Lord Almighty, if you will only look on your servant's misery and remember me, and not forget your servant but give her a son, then I will give him to the Lord for all the days of his life, and no razor will ever be used on his head.'

CHAPTER EIGHT: THE PRAYERS OF A PRINCESS

As she kept on praying to the Lord, Eli observed her mouth. Hannah was praying in her heart, and her lips were moving but her voice was not heard." (1 Samuel 1:10-13a, NIV)

Hannah prayed so intensely, Eli, the priest, thought she was drunk. She understood that prayer was her opportunity to pour out the concerns of her heart to the only One who could do something about them.

She explained to the priest, *"I am a woman who is deeply troubled. I have not been drinking wine or beer; I was pouring out my soul to the Lord. Do not take your servant for a wicked woman; I have been praying here out of my great anguish and grief."* (1 Samuel 1:15-16, NIV)

Notice how Hannah's prayer fits the pattern shown in Jesus' example. Hannah's prayer was **persistent**—year after year she worshiped and sacrificed to God with her husband (see 1 Samuel 1:3). Her prayer was **purposeful** and specific—she asked God to remember her and give her a son (see 1 Samuel 1:11). Her prayer was **persuasive**—she made a vow to God, saying she would give the son back to Him if He would bless her with a child. And her prayer was **powerful**—before the next year's sacrifice, Hannah gave birth to the son she requested.

The King heard the prayer of His daughter, saw her anguish, responded to her need, showed His power and received the glory through this praying princess' powerful prayers.

The Power of Prayer

Prayer has the power to overcome enemies (see Psalm 6:9-10), conquer death (see 2 Kings 4:3-36), bring about healing (see James 5:14-15), and defeat demons (see Mark 9:29). God, through prayer, opens eyes, changes hearts, heals wounds, and grants wisdom (see James 1:5). The power of prayer should never be underestimated because it draws on the glory and might of the infinitely powerful God of the universe!

When we begin to see results from praying like this, we too will be encouraged to tap into the true power of prayer. We will begin to see God doing the miraculous in the spiritual realm. God will begin to show you His might and strength in ways you have never seen before!

CHAPTER EIGHT: THE PRAYERS OF A PRINCESS

Priceless Pearl

"Whatever you ask in my name, this I will do, that the Father may be glorified in the Son. If you ask me anything in my name, I will do it."
John 14:13-14

Princess Proclamation

I have been given access to the throne of the King of Kings through prayer. When boldly I approach His throne in faith, I find the help I need in my time of trouble.

I can ask God to meet my needs. I can ask God for what I want. If I ask Him anything according to His will, it is mine.

It pleases God to answer my prayers. He gives His children

good things and satisfies our desires.

I do not doubt God's ability to work on my behalf.

I can see many examples of God's goodness to me.

Even as I am praying He is already at work because He knows my thoughts before I ask Him.

God will answer my prayers in His own way and in His timing, which is perfect.

He has my best interests at heart.

I trust Him completely.

CHAPTER EIGHT: THE PRAYERS OF A PRINCESS

HIGHEST PRAISE

I will magnify You Lord and give You glory.
I will lift my hands and bless Your holy name.
When the saints shall gather in the sanctuary
By Your spirit You inhabit every praise.

With my whole heart I will worship Your name.
With my spirit, give You glory and praise.
With my life, Lord, for the rest of my days.
For the Lord alone deserves the highest praise.

Hallelujah!

Let us magnify the Lord and give Him glory.
Let us lift our hands and bless His holy name.
When the saints shall gather in the sanctuary
By His spirit He inhabits every praise.

With my whole heart I will worship Your name.
With my spirit, give You glory and praise.

With my life, Lord, for the rest of my days.
For the Lord alone deserves the highest praise.

We adore You;
Bow before You.
For the Lord is great and greatly to be praised!
Oh, bless His name!

Hallelujah!

We'll magnify the Lord someday in glory.
We will lift our hands and bless His holy name.
Where the saints will gather and we'll tell the story.
By His spirit He inhabits every praise.

With my whole heart I will worship Your name.
With my spirit, give You glory and praise.
With my life, Lord, for the rest of my days.
For the Lord alone deserves the highest praise.

Hallelujah!

9

The Praises of a Princess

"Only in the act of praise and worship can a person learn to believe in the goodness and greatness of God."
—C.S. Lewis

"I will bless the LORD at all times; His praise shall continually be in my mouth."
—Psalm 34:1, KJV

The Purpose of Praise

*I*f prayer is a conversation, then praise is a monologue.

Praise is offered to God as an expression of our love, honor, devotion and gratitude for who He is and for the awesome things He has done. Praise is an outpouring of genuine, sincere admiration for our Heavenly Father, the King.

"Most Christians believe that praising God and being thankful is good; however, many think it is optional, something to do after they have served the Lord in other ways. Some Christians only praise God when their circumstances are good and they have a reason to thank Him. The truth is that praising God is not an option. Praise has a powerful effect on the believer, the devil, and on God. It is our highest calling." — Andrew Wommack

If we truly understood the purpose, process, profits and the power of praise, then we would realize it is not optional in the life of a true Daughter of the King. It is mandatory. This is because praise has a tremendous impact on activities of the spirit realm, where God operates on our behalf.

The Process of Praise

The process of praise can be no more beautifully illustrated than throughout the book of Psalms. King David, whom the Bible calls a "man after God's own heart" wrote an entire book of the Bible full of songs of praise to God. David understood that the act of praise was an effective way to chronicle his experiences and God's responses. He recorded his praise and worship to God in 150 chapters of this book of songs, which we can and should frequently use as part of our worship to the King.

The process of praise can be summarized through the acronym **P.R.A.I.S.E:**

💎 ***"P" is for "Promote."*** When we praise God, we are essentially acting as God's P.R. agents, responsible for promoting His name in the earth. Our job is to brag about God so that people who do not know Him will be introduced to Him through our personal testimonies of His goodness. *"Shout for joy to God, all the earth! Sing the glory of his name; make his praise glorious." (Psalm 66:1-2 NIV)*

CHAPTER NINE: THE PRAISES OF A PRINCESS

💎 **"R" is for "Rejoice."** We are to celebrate who God is, as well as what He has done. *"Come and see what God has done, his awesome deeds for mankind!" (Psalm 66:5 NIV)*

💎 **"A" is for "Acclaim."** Through praise, we enthusiastically and publicly express to God how much we appreciate Him. We remind Him of how special He is to us. *"All the earth bows down to you..." (Psalm 66:4a NIV)*

💎 **"I" is for "Invite."** We welcome the presence of God into our situations when we praise. God is drawn to our praise. It is like sweet-smelling incense that rises to heaven and gets His attention. As a matter of fact, God lives in our praise. *"But thou art holy, O thou that inhabitest the praises of Israel" (Psalm 22:3 KJV).* The Hebrew word translated "inhabit" means "to dwell, to remain, to sit." In the midst of our praise is where God desires to be. And praise draws Him close to us.

💎 **"S" is for "Sing."** The act of singing is a tremendously important and powerful part of praising God. *"Sing the glory of his name..." (Psalm 66:2a NIV) "...they sing praise to you, they sing the praises of your name" (Psalm 66:4b NIV).* Whether or not we have natural musical talent, singing praises to God lifts our spirits and helps us to easily recall what He has done in our lives. *"...be filled with the Spirit, speaking to one another with psalms, hymns, and songs from the Spirit. Sing and make music from your heart to the Lord. (Ephesians 5:18b-19 NIV)*

💎 **"E" is for "Every Day."** Praise should be incorporated into our daily time of prayer and worship to the Lord. *"By him therefore let us offer the sacrifice of praise to God continually, that is, the fruit of our lips giving thanks to his name" (Hebrews 13:15 KJV).* Each and every day we need to find something for which we can be thankful. Just the fact that we woke up today is worthy of praise to God! *"...always giving thanks to God the Father for everything, in* the name of our Lord Jesus Christ." (Ephesians 5:20 NIV)

The Profits of Praise

There are many benefits of praising and worshipping God.

Praise lifts our spirits, taking our minds off our problems and helping us to focus on God. Praise encourages others who hear us talk about God's goodness. People expect us to be discouraged when we encounter difficulties. But when we continue to bless the Lord through and despite our challenges, our impact is greatest among our observers. *"Let the redeemed of the Lord tell their story—those he redeemed from the hand of the foe." (Psalm 107:2 NIV)*

Praise causes you to shift your focus from the size of your problems to the size of your God. *"You will keep in perfect peace those whose minds are steadfast, because they trust in you." (Isaiah 26:3 NIV)*

Praise will increase your spiritual strength and uphold you during difficult times. *"For the joy of the LORD is your strength." (Nehemiah 8:1b KJV)*

Praise transforms our countenance. It can even alter our physical appearance. Praise can remove the worry and frown lines from a stressed woman's face and replace it with the soft smile of a woman assured. *"Rejoice in the LORD, righteous ones; for the praise of the upright is beautiful." (Psalm 33:1, ISV)* *"Praise the LORD! For it is good to sing praises to our God, for it is pleasant and praise is becoming." (Psalm 147:1, NASB)*

A Praising Princess

When Hannah witnessed first-hand the awesome power of the King in the miraculous way He answered her prayers for a son, all she could do was praise God. The book of 1 Samuel chapter 2 records the praises of this princess.

As she reflected on the shame she experienced both internally (she was barren) and externally (she was taunted by her husband's second wife), and how God had blessed and exalted her, Hannah uttered one of the most beautiful songs of praise recorded in the Bible (read 1 Samuel 2:1-10).

"*Then Hannah prayed and said: 'My heart rejoices in the Lord; in the Lord my horn is lifted high. My mouth boasts over my enemies, for I delight in your deliverance. There is no one holy like the Lord; there is no one besides you; there is no Rock like our God.'*" (1 Samuel 2:1-2, NIV)

Notice how Hannah's prayer praise fits the pattern of praise. First, she **promotes** the name of God. She gives Him all the credit (1 Samuel 2:1). Second, she **rejoices**. She "delights" in God's deliverance (1 Samuel 2:2). Third, she **acclaims** God. She publicly exalts Him, saying "there is no Rock like our God" (1 Samuel 2:2b). She **invites** God into her situation through her praise. She **sings** a song of victory over the enemies of depression, despair and discouragement. Hannah's great love for God and for the son she so desperately desired served as constant reminders of the awesome power the King chose to display in the life of His daughter.

The Power of Praise

Praise confuses the devil. When the Israelites went to battle against Jericho, it was their praise that brought down the walls and enabled them to capture the city (see Joshua 6:20). When Job was tested by sudden disaster and devastation, it was his praise to God that confounded Satan's plan (see Job 13:15). When the Moabites and Ammonites came against Jehoshaphat and the children of Israel, it was the act of praise which defeated their enemies (see 2 Chronicles 20:21-24).

Praise to God literally transforms our environment. "*Indeed it came to pass, when the trumpeters and singers were as one, to make one sound to be heard in praising and thanking the LORD, and when they lifted up their voice with the trumpets and cymbals and instruments of music, and praised the LORD, saying: 'For He* is good, For His mercy endures forever,' that the house, the house of the LORD, was filled with a cloud, so that the priests could not continue ministering because of the cloud; for the glory of the LORD filled the house of God." (2 Chronicles 5:13-14, NKJV)

Hallelujah Anyhow

We don't need to "feel" like praising God or be in a good mood in order to praise Him. Praise is not dependent on our emotions. Regardless of how we feel, God is forever worthy of praise. Praise is an attitude, a mindset, and an act of our will, which when genuinely offered to the Lord, always results in an emotional shift. When we praise God even when we don't feel like it, we will feel like it after we've praised Him. Always. 100% Praise Back Guaranteed. Try it!

Whether we sing songs, clap our hands, or even leap for joy, the ways we can praise God are endless. May God's daughters remember to always give glory and passionate praise to our King for who He is and for the great things He has done.

He is worthy of our praise!

CHAPTER NINE: THE PRAISES OF A PRINCESS

Priceless Pearl

"I will bless the LORD at all times; His praise shall continually be in my mouth."
Psalm 34:1

Princess Proclamation

I will bless the Lord at all times.
His praise shall continually be in my mouth. My soul boasts of God's unlimited power.
God is good! He's good to me!
I reflect on the awesome things only God could do in my life and I give Him full credit. I had nothing to do with my success. It is all His doing.

Even in my failures, God is the one who softens the blows.
I have never experienced the consequences I deserve. He pities me. He has compassion on me. He is ever merciful.
For these things I praise Him.
I praise Him not only for what He's done, but just for who He is.
He is the Ruler of the whole earth. There is no one greater.
My soul bows down in humility.
I bow in awe and worship my King.

CHAPTER NINE: THE PRAISES OF A PRINCESS

Lyrical Love Letter

MY SOUL'S PRAISE

I love You, adore You.
I bow down before You.
I lift my hands in holy praise
Because of who You are.

You're the Living Water in dry land.
Emmanuel, the Great I AM,
Messiah, Christ and Elohim
Are who You claimed to be.
And I sing out to thee!

You are so Wonderful!
You are the Counselor.
You are the Mighty God.
You are the Prince of Peace.
My soul cries out...

To the Savior who was crucified;
To the Morning Star that shines so bright;

S. Kristi Douglas

The sweetest smell of Sharon's Rose
It all comes from You.
You're the Lily of the Valley.
You're the King of Kings and LORD of Lords,
The Mediator and the Door
That I came through.
And now I sing to You!

You are so Wonderful!
You are the Counselor.
You are the Mighty God.
You are the Prince of Peace.
You are my Savior.
You bled and died for me.
You hung there on the tree.
My soul cries out to thee.
My soul cries out...

Oh, for a thousand tongues to sing
The glories of my Lord and King!
No matter what we call Your name,
Age to age you're still the same.
Jesus, You're all the world to me.
That's why I lift my voice to sing.
I will forever bless your name because you are so

Wonderful!
You are the Counselor.
You are the Mighty God.
You are the Prince of Peace.
You are my Savior.
You bled and died for me.
You hung there on the tree.

Chapter Nine: The Praises of a Princess

My soul cries out to thee!
My soul, my soul, my soul cries out to thee!

10

The Passions of a Princess

"If you can't figure out your purpose, figure out your passion.
For your passion will lead you right into your purpose."
–Bishop T.D. Jakes

"Those who live passionately teach us how to love. Those who
love passionately teach us how to live."
–Sarah Ban Breathnach

"I hunger for Your love.
I'm thirsty for Your touch.
I've heard about the things You've done.
With two fish and loaves of bread
five thousand men were fed.
Would You do it all again
just for one?"
–S. Kristi Douglas, "Satisfy My Soul"

CHAPTER TEN: THE PASSIONS OF A PRINCESS

The sun shone brightly against the burning sand. It was noon and she still had chores to complete. Day after day, bearing a heavy pot on her shoulders, she came here to draw water. Typically, women drew from Jacob's Well in the mornings and the evenings, when it was much cooler. But she was hardly a typical woman. And she was in no mood to socialize with the crowd. She had seen their critical stares. She heard what they said behind her back. She knew she'd find no friendship or loyalty among them.

As a matter of fact, she'd grown used to rejection. Divorced by five husbands and living with another man to whom she was not married, she had perfected emotional detachment. There was no way she would allow herself to feel her latent need for genuine love and deep connection when she would inevitably be disappointed by loss.

Women of her day couldn't survive without being married. They needed a man to provide for them and to validate them socially. But she was different. She was a survivor. She'd do whatever it took to make it—even if society disagreed with her methods.

As she drew closer, she saw him sitting by the well. He seemed out of place. What was he doing here? She could tell he was Jewish. She was a Samaritan. Her people and the Jews were like oil and water—they just didn't mix. Besides, men and women who were strangers never spoke casually. Yet, there was something in this man's eyes which spoke to her soul loud and clear. He was different from the other men. His gaze was kind and familiar, as if he were waiting for her arrival. It made her uncomfortable.

"Get it together," she thought, in an effort to dismiss her unease. "Draw the water and hurry back home. You have more to be worried about than this stranger."

And then he spoke. *"Will you give me a drink?"*

She was stunned when she heard his voice. "You are a Jew and I am a Samaritan woman. How can you ask me for a drink?" she asked. Not only was he crossing racial lines by speaking to her, but he broke gender and religious barriers too.

John 4 tells the full story of their encounter.

Jesus answered her, "If you knew the gift of God and who it is that asks you for a drink, you would have asked him and he would have given you living water."

"Sir," the woman said, "you have nothing to draw with and the well is deep. Where can you get this living water? Are you greater than our father Jacob, who gave us the well and drank from it himself, as did also his sons and his livestock?"

Jesus answered, "Everyone who drinks this water will be thirsty again, but whoever drinks the water I give them will never thirst. Indeed, the water I give them will become in them a spring of water welling up to eternal life."

The woman said to him, "Sir, give me this water so that I won't get thirsty and have to keep coming here to draw water."

He told her, "Go, call your husband and come back."

"I have no husband," she replied.

Jesus said to her, "You are right when you say you have no husband. The fact is, you have had five husbands, and the man you now have is not your husband. What you have just said is quite true."

"Sir," the woman said, "I can see that you are a prophet. Our ancestors worshiped on this mountain, but you Jews claim that the place where we must worship is in Jerusalem."

"Woman," Jesus replied, "believe me, a time is coming when you will worship the Father neither on this mountain nor in Jerusalem. You Samaritans worship what you do not know; we worship what we do know, for salvation is from the Jews. Yet a time is coming and has now come when the true worshipers will worship the Father in the Spirit and in truth, for they are the kind of worshipers the Father seeks. God is spirit, and his worshipers must worship in the Spirit and in truth."

CHAPTER TEN: THE PASSIONS OF A PRINCESS

The woman said, "I know that Messiah" (called Christ) "is coming. When he comes, he will explain everything to us." Then Jesus declared, "I, the one speaking to you—I am he."

Just then his disciples returned and were surprised to find him talking with a woman. But no one asked, "What do you want?" or "Why are you talking with her?"

Then, leaving her water jar, the woman went back to the town and said to the people, "Come, see a man who told me everything I ever did. Could this be the Messiah?" They came out of the town and made their way toward him.

Many of the Samaritans from that town believed in him because of the woman's testimony, "He told me everything I ever did." So when the Samaritans came to him, they urged him to stay with them, and he stayed two days. And because of his words many more became believers.

They said to the woman, "We no longer believe just because of what you said; now we have heard for ourselves, and we know that this man really is the Savior of the world." (John 4:10-42, NIV)

A Woman of Great Passion

Passion has been described as "putting more energy into something than is required." It is what drives, motivates and compels us to action or feeling. Passion is fueled by a deep hunger, unfulfilled desire or need for more.

The woman at the well was there to meet a natural, recurring need. Her intent was to draw water to satisfy her physical thirst. Yet, her encounter with Christ exposed within her a more desperate thirst.

Because of her experiences with failed relationships, she became spiritually depleted. Repeated disappointments and rejection made her emotionally dehydrated. Her soul was thirsty.

In the book of Psalms, David shares a similar sentiment. *"You, God, are my God, earnestly I seek you; I thirst for you, my whole* being longs for you, in a dry and parched land where there is no water." (Psalm 63:1, NIV).

David realized that his need for spiritual fulfillment could only be met by God. Likewise, Jesus identified the woman's need for spiritual hydration, a need that only He could fill.

"If you knew the gift of God and who it is that asks you for a drink, you would have asked him and he would have given you living water."

Intrigued by the prospect of something that could both give life and quench thirst, the woman, who was spiritually dead, asked, "Where can you get this living water?"

That's exactly what an encounter with Jesus does. When we are introduced to God in the flesh—the One who at once gives life, yet is Life, and who created water and yet is Water personified—we are confronted with our own emptiness and thirst.

Jesus answered, "Everyone who drinks this water will be thirsty again, but whoever drinks the water I give them will never thirst. Indeed, the water I give them will become in them a spring of water welling up to eternal life."

When we stand before Christ, we realize how great our need is for Him. An encounter with Jesus makes our thirst for Him even greater.

CHAPTER TEN: THE PASSIONS OF A PRINCESS

The woman said to him, *"Sir, give me this water so that I won't get thirsty and have to keep coming here to draw water."*

The woman recognized her recurring need. Day after day she lifted and carried the heavy pots full of water to and fro. And yet she knew that what she collected would only last her until the next day. It was a never-ending cycle. She was intrigued and excited by Christ's offer to fill her need once and for all.

She had tried five times unsuccessfully to fill her void. Now, she would try a sixth time to make it work.

Many people ridiculed this woman for her lifestyle. Even today, some might criticize her for having been married five times. However, a woman in her day needed to be married in order to have her needs met. She could not independently provide for herself. This woman had legitimate financial, physical, relational and emotional needs which she believed could not be met in any other way.

Before we become too critical, look closely. We might find that we, too, have had several "husbands." Consider this as honestly as you can. Over the course of your lifetime, when you are feeling empty, discouraged, depressed, depleted—thirsty—what have you used to fill the voids (emotional, physical, spiritual) in your life?

Anything that we put in place of God becomes an offense to Him. *"Thou shalt have no other gods before me"* (Exodus 20:3, KJV). When we idolize something or someone, God then allows us to become even more dissatisfied than we were before we used it. He exposes the weaknesses and flaws in those activities so that we will see how futile they are when compared to the one true source of our spiritual fulfillment.

"My people have committed two sins: They have forsaken me, the spring of living water, and have dug their own cisterns, broken cisterns that cannot hold water." (Jeremiah 2:13, NIV)

Can you imagine what would have happened if the woman at the well lugged a cracked pot back and forth? She would fill it up only to lose it all on the way home!

If we believe things or relationships can satisfy us, then we are truly cracked pots relying on cracked pots!

As ridiculous as it sounds, that's exactly what we do. When we choose something (or someone) other than God to fill our voids (and we all have them), we are using leaky, ineffective containers. And while we may experience temporary satisfaction, we will become more thirsty and exhausted from having to repeat the act over and over and over again.

That is why Jesus told the woman, *"Everyone who drinks this water will be thirsty again, but whoever drinks the water I give them will never thirst. Indeed, the water I give them will become in them a spring of water welling up to eternal life."*

We will never be satisfied with anything other than a true relationship with Jesus.

He is the only one who can satisfy our souls. He is the Living Water. When we continuously draw from the deep well of the word of God, saturating ourselves in prayer and meditation, we will find that a relationship with Christ quenches our deepest desires and relieves our thirst for more. We will wonder why we ever sought out anything else.

"As the deer pants for streams of water, so my soul pants for you, my God. My soul thirsts for God, for the living God. When can I go and meet with God?" (Psalm 42:1-2, NIV)

David's desperate plea is answered by Christ himself. The same gift He offered to the woman at the well is offered to the Daughters of the King:

"Blessed are those who hunger and thirst for righteousness, for they will be filled." (Matthew 5:6, NIV)

Chapter Ten: The Passions of a Princess

Priceless Pearl

"Blessed are those who hunger and thirst for righteousness, for they will be filled."
Matthew 5:6

Princess Proclamation

I hunger for God's love.
I thirst for God's touch.
There is no other who can heal the broken places of my heart.
God is the only one whose love truly satisfies me.
I run to Him in times of trouble. He is my healer.
He is the living water who quenches my thirst.
I want more of Him.

S. Kristi Douglas

I need more of His Holy Spirit to fill me.
I put no one else before Him.
He is my God.

CHAPTER TEN: THE PASSIONS OF A PRINCESS

Lyrical Love Letter

SATISFY MY SOUL

I hunger for Your love.
I'm thirsty for Your touch.
I've heard about the things You've done.
With two fish and loaves of bread
Five thousand men were fed.
Would You do it all again, just for one?

Satisfy my soul.
Savior, let me know
That this hunger in my heart
Can only be filled by You alone.
Let me taste and see
How good You are to me.
And the quenching of my thirst
Can only come when I put You first.
Oh, Savior won't you satisfy my soul?

I searched for an embrace
To fill this empty space.

Found nothing can replace Your spirit.
Now, You're all I desire
So come and take me higher.
Rekindle holy fire within me!

Satisfy my soul.
Savior, let me know
That this hunger in my heart
Can only be filled by You alone.
Let me taste and see
How good You are to me.
And the quenching of my thirst
Can only come when I put You first.
Oh, Savior won't you satisfy?

Lord, I must confess that this emptiness
Comes from trying to fill my broken heart
With something less.
Said that You could heal the longing that I feel.
Oh, Bread of Life and Living Water come and now fulfill!

Satisfy my soul.
Savior, let me know
That this hunger in my heart
Can only be filled by You alone.
Let me taste and see
How good You are to me.
And the quenching of my thirst
Can only come when I put You first.

Satisfy my soul.
Savior, now I know
That this hunger in my heart

Can only be filled by You alone.
Let me taste and see
How good You've been to me.
To You I give this empty cup.
Only You can fill me up.
Refresh my spirit and make me whole.
Savior, won't You satisfy my soul?

Only You can satisfy my soul.

11

The Possibilities of a Princess

"For I know the plans I have for you," declares the LORD, "plans to prosper you and not to harm you, plans to give you hope and a future."
—Jeremiah 29:11, NIV)

Nothing is impossible.
The word itself says "I'm possible!"
—Audrey Hepburn

"Then the Lord said to Abraham, 'Why did Sarah laugh and say, "Will I really have a child, now that I am old?" Is anything too hard for the Lord?'"
—Genesis 18:13-14a, NIV

Chapter Eleven: The Possibilities of a Princess

His tiny toes. His button nose. The way his little fist curled around her pointer finger as he nursed. She adored everything about him. Drawing him closely to her breast, she stuck her nose into the crease of his neck and inhaled deeply. She could hardly get enough of his newborn scent. She had always adored children. And they, too, loved the way she doted on and spoiled them as if they belonged to her. Yet, this child was different from the others.

After 90 years of dreams dashed and prayers paused, he was one she could finally call her own.

She laughed in disbelief when the angel told her that she would conceive a son. Who would ever believe that an old woman could experience such joy? As she cuddled her son, Isaac, whose name meant "laughter," she recalled God's goodness in keeping His promise to her. The wife of Abraham, the mother of Isaac, and the grandmother of Jacob—the founding fathers of the Jewish faith—would eventually become the mother of God's chosen people.

Princess, do you ever dare to dream about the possibilities God has in store for you? Perhaps you believe God has given you a vision or a desire for something far greater than what exists now. You realize that it is beyond your own power to obtain. Like this woman, you've been harboring hope for as long as you can remember, yet God has not allowed you to see it come to pass.

What do we do when we believe we've heard from God, yet because of the magnitude of the vision or the amount of time we've been praying and hoping, our faith begins to fail? How can we be sure of God's will?

"Be assured: you can know God's will, and you can know it for sure. The Lord does not play games with His children by hiding His thoughts from us. One of His greatest desires for us is that we live out His plan for our lives." —Dr. Charles Stanley

Understanding God's Will

When we consider our desires and the possibilities before us, there are some questions we must ask ourselves.

◆ **Is it in line with the word of God?** God will never violate His word in order to give us what we want. We need to look for scripture that will confirm or deny whether we are heading in the right direction. Sometimes we cannot find a scripture which relates to an exact subject. But the word of God is based on principles that apply to many circumstances. Let scripture be your guide but ask the Holy Spirit for wisdom that applies specifically to your situation. *"All Scripture is God-breathed and is useful for teaching, rebuking, correcting and training in righteousness, so that the servant of God may be thoroughly equipped for every good work."* (2 Timothy 3:16-17, NIV)

◆ **Is this a wise thing to do?** Ask yourself if you feel pressured or rushed into doing this. Have you thought through all the steps? How will this affect your future? Will anyone be harmed if you do this? Remember that God wants the best for everyone involved (see Romans 8:28), not just you. So consider the big picture.

◆ **Am I at peace with this decision?** Some Christians say they feel free to move forward because they have "prayed about it." But you must allow God the freedom to redirect your steps if He chooses (see Proverbs 3:5-6). Be sure that you are completely at ease before you move forward. If you are not, then you should pause before proceeding. *"We can make our plans, but the LORD determines our steps."* (Proverbs 16:9, NLT)

◆ **Does this demonstrate the characteristics of a Daughter of the King?** Are you doing anything that would cause you or others physical or spiritual harm? Is your testimony at stake? Would others think less of God because of this action? If so, you might con-

Chapter Eleven: The Possibilities of a Princess

sider whether this is actually God's will for you. Our actions and attitudes should reflect an obedient heart toward God. This should be our greatest priority, rather than considering our own desires. *"Or didn't you realize that your body is a sacred place, the place of the Holy Spirit? Don't you see that you can't live however you please, squandering what God paid such a high price for? The physical part of you is not some piece of property belonging to the spiritual part of you. God owns the whole works. So let people see God in and through your body."* (1 Corinthians 6:19-20, MSG)

♦ **Does this fit God's purpose for my life?** Based on what you know about God's word, character and specific instructions to you, consider whether this decision aligns with God's long-range plans for your life. God knows all and sees all circumstances (see Jeremiah 29:11). He is working all things together for your good.

When we honestly answer these questions, we will discover the will of God. We must be willing to act in obedience, by faith, once we understand what God wants for our lives. We should desire to say, as Jesus said, *"I have brought you glory on earth by finishing the work you gave me to do." (John 17:4, NIV)*

The Promotion of a Princess

Much of Bible history can be traced back to the woman whom God used mightily to do the impossible. Sarai, or "Princess," was her birth name. But God eventually changed her name to "Sarah," for He had elevated her to the status of a queen. *"I will bless her so that she will be the mother of nations; kings of peoples will come from her." (Genesis 17:16b, NIV)*

Because of her faith, God promoted her. He gave her more than she ever hoped for because she believed in His ability to do the impossible.

"And by faith even Sarah, who was past childbearing age, was enabled to bear children because she considered him faithful who had made the promise." (Hebrews 11:11, NIV).

At 90 years of age, Sarah was well past normal childbearing years. Notice that it was her faith which gave her the capacity to give birth. Her faith put into action the very thing which God had already promised. There are two active participants in the will of God: God and us. And nothing can happen without both working together.

Sometimes having to wait on God can cause our faith to falter. This is why scripture encourages us, *"Let us not become weary in doing good, for at the proper time we will reap a harvest if we do not give up." (Galatians 6:9 NIV)* Waiting on God increases our strength (see Psalm 27:13-14 and Isaiah 40:31).

Once we are sure that what we hope and pray for is truly the will of God, like Sarah, there are three things we must do in order to receive strength to realize the possibilities God desires for us.

◆ **Recall God's provision.** The best indicator of what God will do for us in the future is what He has done in the past. David wrote, *"My soul is downcast within me; therefore I will remember*

CHAPTER ELEVEN: THE POSSIBILITIES OF A PRINCESS

you..." *(Psalm 42:6a NIV)*. When we think about how God has provided for us, delivered us out of trouble or answered prayer, we become encouraged that He can and will do it again. *"I will remember the deeds of the LORD; yes, I will remember your miracles of long ago." (Psalm 77:11, NIV)*

♦ **Remember God's promise.** We must continually remind ourselves of what God said He would do for us. *"Remember your promise to me; it is my only hope" (Psalm 119:49, NLT)*. The enemy wants to convince us that we are forgotten. However, God is simply waiting for us to acknowledge His word of promise to us. *"...I am watching over my word to perform it." (Jeremiah 1:12b, ESV)*

♦ **Rejoice over God's plans.** God already knows that wonderful things are ahead and the best is yet to come (see Jeremiah 29:11). Even the unpleasant things that happen to us still work out for our good (see Romans 8:28). We can't even imagine what God has in store (see Ephesians 3:20). Praise God in advance for what He's about to do!

Daughter of the King, you must know and believe this with all your heart: there is nothing too hard for God.

With God, **nothing is impossible**.

All things are possible with God.

Priceless Pearl

"For I know the plans I have for you," declares the LORD, "plans to prosper you and not to harm you, plans to give you hope and a future."
Jeremiah 29:11

Princess Proclamation

My purpose is clear.
I am prepared for such a time as this.
I have been purified for God's use.
The promises of God are mine.
I have been given supernatural power to defeat the enemy.
God hears my prayers.

CHAPTER ELEVEN: THE POSSIBILITIES OF A PRINCESS

God receives my praise.
The King desires to fulfill my passions for His glory.
With God nothing is impossible.
All things are possible with God.
Amen.

I CAN DO ALL THINGS

Father Abraham was one
Whom You promised a son.
By a miracle his wife conceived –
A heritage begun.
And that's when he heard Your voice
And he had to make a choice.
Would he lay his son upon the altar?
Trust Your word or would he falter?
As he raised his hands in praise
I hear him say,

"I can do all things
through God who strengthens me.
No matter what the test
Or how impossible it seems.
For there is nothing too hard for God
if only I believe.
I can do all things
Through God who strengthens me."

Chapter Eleven: The Possibilities of a Princess

Now I walk this lonely road
Bearing such a precious load.
As I look ahead I see
The sacrifice required of me.
And that's when I hear Your voice
And I have to make the choice.
To lay my all upon this altar,
Trust Your word or will I falter?
And deep within I hear my spirit say,

"I can do all things
through Christ who strengthens me.
No matter what the test
Or how impossible it seems.
For there is nothing too hard for God
if only I believe.
I can do all things
Through God who strengthens me."

Though wearied by the journey,
When it seems I can't go on,
That's when I hear you whisper,
"Let the weak say, 'I am strong.'"

I can do all things
through Christ who strengthens me.
I yield my life because
There's resurrection pow'r in thee.
And there is no thing too hard for God.
Surely I believe
I can do all things through Christ who strengthens.
I'll cling to His power within.
All things through Christ who strengthens me!

Portrait of a Princess Appendix

Debut CD from S. Kristi Douglas
Featuring the title track,
"Daughter of the King"
"Highest Praise"
"Satisfy My Soul"
and more...

Available online @

DOWNLOAD CARD

To redeem your code go to
www.nwdownload.com

YOUR DOWNLOAD CODE IS:

SDUA4SQRNV

NWdownload.com

THE ROYAL DECREE

My Dear Princess:

◈ You may not know me, but I know everything about you
PSALM 139:1

◈ I know when you sit down and when you rise up
PSALM 139:2

◈ I am familiar with all your ways
PSALM 139:3

◈ Even the very hairs on your head are numbered
MATTHEW 10:29-31

◈ For you were made in my image
GENESIS 1:27

◈ In me you live and move and have your being
ACTS 17:28

◈ For you are my offspring
ACTS 17:28

◈ I knew you even before you were conceived
JEREMIAH 1:4-5

◈ I chose you when I planned creation
EPHESIANS 1:11-12

Appendix: The Royal Decree

❖ You were not a mistake
Psalm 139:15-16

❖ For all your days are written in my book
Psalm 139:15-16

❖ I determined the exact time of your birth and where you would live
Acts 17:26

❖ You are fearfully and wonderfully made
Psalm 139:14

❖ I knit you together in your mother's womb
Psalm 139:13

❖ And brought you forth on the day you were born
Psalm 71:6

❖ I have been misrepresented by those who don't know me
John 8:41-44

❖ I am not distant and angry, but am the complete expression of love
1 John 4:16

❖ And it is my desire to lavish my love on you
1 John 3:1

◆ Simply because you are my child and I am your Father
1 JOHN 3:1

◆ I offer you more than your earthly father ever could
MATTHEW 7:11

◆ For I am the perfect Father
MATTHEW 5:48

◆ Every good gift that you receive comes from my hand
JAMES 1:17

◆ For I am your provider and I meet all your needs
MATTHEW 6:31-33

◆ My plan for your future has always been filled with hope
JEREMIAH 29:11

◆ Because I love you with an everlasting love
JEREMIAH 31:3

◆ My thoughts toward you are countless as the sand on the seashore
PSALM 139:17-18

◆ And I rejoice over you with singing
ZEPHANIAH 3:17

APPENDIX: THE ROYAL DECREE

❖ I will never stop doing good to you
JEREMIAH 32:40

❖ For you are my treasured possession
EXODUS 19:5

❖ I desire to establish you with all my heart and all my soul
JEREMIAH 32:41

❖ And I want to show you great and marvelous things
JEREMIAH 33:3

❖ If you seek me with all your heart, you will find me
DEUTERONOMY 4:29

❖ Delight in me and I will give you the desires of your heart
PSALM 37:4

❖ For it is I who gave you those desires
PHILIPPIANS 2:13

❖ I am able to do more for you than you could imagine
EPHESIANS 3:20

❖ For I am your greatest encourager
2 THESSALONIANS 2:16-17

❖ I am also the Father who comforts you in all your troubles
2 CORINTHIANS 1:3-4

💎 When you are brokenhearted, I am close to you
PSALM 34:18

💎 As a shepherd carries a lamb, I have carried you close to my heart
ISAIAH 40:11

💎 One day I will wipe away every tear from your eyes
REVELATION 21:3-4

💎 And I'll take away all the pain you have suffered on this earth
REVELATION 21:4

💎 I am your Father and I love you even as I love my son, Jesus
JOHN 17:23

💎 For in Jesus my love for you is revealed
JOHN 17:26

💎 He is the exact representation of my being
HEBREWS 1:3

💎 And He came to demonstrate that I am for you, not against you
ROMANS 8:31

💎 And to tell you that I am not counting your sins
2 CORINTHIANS 5:18-19

Appendix: The Royal Decree

❖ Jesus died so that you and I could be reconciled
2 CORINTHIANS 5:18-19

❖ His death was the ultimate expression of my love for you
1 JOHN 4:10

❖ I gave up everything I loved that I might gain your love
ROMANS 8:32

❖ If you receive the gift of my son Jesus, you receive me
1 JOHN 2:23

❖ And nothing will ever separate you from my love again
ROMANS 8:38-39

❖ Come home and I'll throw the biggest party heaven has ever seen
LUKE 15:7

❖ I have always been Father and will always be Father
EPHESIANS 3:14-15

❖ My question is, will you be My child? I am waiting for you
JOHN 1:12-13; LUKE 15:11-32

Love Always,
Your Heavenly Father,

The King of Kings

Royal Retreat Study Guide

Appendix: Study Guide

Introduction

"We break down every thought and proud thing that puts itself up against the wisdom of God. We take hold of every thought and make it obey Christ."
—1 Corinthians 10:5, NLV

"Daughter of the King, if you have given your life to Christ, you, too, have been spiritually born into a royal family. This means that you have been granted a supernatural birth right to rule and reign in the spirit realm. You, too, have been afforded certain privileges simply because you are God's child."
—S. Kristi Douglas

"Princess, take your rightful place in the kingdom of God. This can only happen when you begin to understand what God says about you. You must learn the truth about who you are from The King's point of view. But most importantly, you must believe it!"
—S. Kristi Douglas

A Princess Ponders...

Bullies need victims. They don't just pick on anyone. They hand-pick their victims based on their weaknesses, lack of assertiveness and perceived inability to fight back. Bullies can smell fear. Victims, on the other hand, *"...easily acquiesce to the demands of bullies: They cry and assume defensive postures. Not only do they not fight back, they hand over their possessions—handsomely rewarding their attackers psychologically and materially—powerfully reinforcing them."* (Hara Estroff Marano, Editor at Large, Psychology Today)

In our fictional example, the bully threatened his victim when he was vulnerable, unattended, unprotected and invisible to others. Consider the times the devil has "bullied" you into a certain behavior or belief.

1. Which negative behaviors, faulty beliefs or strong temptations most frequently occur to you?

2. What patterns do you notice around the timing of his attacks? Note whether they tend to come at a certain time of day, month, or year. Did they happen before, during or after a certain event? Explain.

3. The bible says we can prepare for the enemy's attacks. Using the following scriptures, what specific actions can you take to protect yourself from the attacks of the devil?

♦ 1 Peter 5:8 —

♦ Psalm 119:11 —

♦ Ephesians 6:10-18 —

♦ Proverbs 18:10 —

♦ Matthew 10:16 —

4. A princess is no ordinary woman. When you think of the word "princess," who comes to mind (real or fictional)? What adjectives would you use to describe her? List as many adjectives as you can. Try to list at least 10, though you'll likely come up with more.

   1.

   2.

   3.

4.

5.

6.

7.

8.

9.

10.

5. A king is no ordinary ruler. When you think of the word "king," who comes to mind (real or fictional)? What adjectives would you use to describe him? List as many adjectives as you can. Try to list at least 10, though you'll likely come up with more.

1.

2.

3.

4.

5.

6.

7.

8.

9.

10.

APPENDIX: STUDY GUIDE

Self-Esteem Check

1. Imagine that the following gauge represents your current level of self-esteem. Mark your current level of self-esteem and today's date on the gauge. (Note: you will find this image and exercise repeated in the remaining study guide lessons.)

2. Why did you place yourself there?

3. Notice that the gauge ranges from Empty ("E") to Full ("F"). How do you define full?

4. Is it possible to be full? Why or why not?

5. What needs to happen in order to move the needle closer to full?

APPENDIX: STUDY GUIDE

Chapter One

Who Do You Think You Are?

"You are a chosen people, a royal priesthood, a holy nation, God's special possession, that you may declare the praises of him who called you out of darkness into his wonderful light."
–1 Peter 2:9

"You may feel unworthy to wear the crown of righteousness which God has appointed for you. But as you align your mind with His word – as you begin to believe and walk out the truth of what you learn – your crown will no longer be at risk of falling. Your acceptance of your royal heritage will become second nature."
–S. Kristi Douglas

"We must shift from a concept of self-esteem to developing a sense of "God-esteem" – the idea that what God says to be true of us (both good and bad) is central to experiencing a life of success and spiritual prosperity."
–S. Kristi Douglas

A Princess Ponders...

1. Read Matthew 7:24-27. Can you think of an instance where you may have built your self-esteem on "sand" (a shifting,

variable platform)?

2. If so, what was the foundation of your thinking? If you cannot think of any instances, ask God to reveal them to you.

3. Can you think of an instance where you may have built your self-esteem on "rock" (a solid, permanent platform)?

4. If so, what was the foundation of your thinking? If you cannot think of any instances, ask God to reveal them to you.

Self-Esteem Check

1. Imagine that the following gauge represents your current level of self-esteem. Mark your current level of self-esteem and today's date on the gauge.

2. Why did you place yourself there?

3. What needs to happen in order to move the needle closer to full?

S. Kristi Douglas

Lyrical Love Letter

Listen to **"Could it Be?"** This song explores the thoughts of a woman who is intrigued by the idea that she could possibly be a daughter of the King. She wonders aloud what God may have in store for her. Have you ever thought about the great things God has planned for your life?

Journal your thoughts after listening to the song.

Chapter Two

A King's Ransom

"It is for freedom that Christ has set us free. Stand firm, then, and do not let yourselves be burdened again by a yoke of slavery."
—Galatians 5:1, NIV

"Although Jesus Christ died to set us free from the power of sin over our lives, many of God's daughters remain spiritually and mentally enslaved. We live as though sin is still our overseer."
—S. Kristi Douglas

"Unable to free ourselves from sin's control, our only hope was a Redeemer who, as 'the Word [who] became flesh' (John 1:14), could Himself become the divine Emancipation Proclamation and decree our spiritual freedom with ultimate authority and finality."
—S. Kristi Douglas

A Princess Ponders...

Once the slaves had been declared free by executive order of the president of the United States of America, they were legally released from obligation to work for their former owners—unless they so desired.

1. Can you recall a time when you were enslaved to sinful habits and wanted to change but felt powerless to do so? What were the circumstances?

2. Did you give in to your desire or were you able to successfully break free? Why or why not?

3. What, if anything, can you do in order to remain free from the power of sin over your life?

4. Can you think of ways in which you have felt responsible for maintaining your own righteousness?

5. Read 2 Corinthians 5:21 and Ephesians 2:8-9. Are you responsible for maintaining your own righteousness? If not, then who is responsible?

6. Read Psalm 119:9-16. What can you do when you are tempted

to return to sinful patterns of behavior from which you know God has delivered you?

7. Although Christ died on the cross to set you free from your sin more than 2,000 years ago, the day you received Christ can be considered your spiritual "Juneteenth." You should be able to recall a specific period of time, and the circumstances under which you were saved. Write the date in the space below. If you don't recall the exact date, write an approximate date. "My spiritual Juneteenth is (day/month), (year)."

Self-Esteem Check

1. Imagine that the following gauge represents your current level of self-esteem. Mark your current level of self-esteem and today's date on the gauge.

2. Why did you place yourself there?

3. What needs to happen in order to move the needle closer to full?

Lyrical Love Letter

Listen to *"The Color of Kings."* This song explains the history of how and why the color purple became a symbol of royalty. Imagine yourself fully dressed in purple regal attire—crown, gown, jewels, scepter, slippers, etc. How do you feel?

Journal your thoughts after listening to the song.

APPENDIX: STUDY GUIDE

Chapter Three
The Purpose of a Princess

"For we are God's masterpiece. He has created us anew in Christ Jesus, so that we can do the good things he planned for us long ago."
–Ephesians 2:10 NLT

"Those who have received Christ have been spiritually born into God's family. Our heavenly Father expects His children to look like Him. The more time we spend with Him in prayer and in reading His word, the more we will begin to think, speak and act like Him. We will begin to 'look' like Him. This pleases God. It's the reason He created us in the first place."
–S. Kristi Douglas

"You are God's masterpiece–His crown jewel; His finest work of art, created specifically in His image. God designed you to be a reflection of Him. Even with all of your flaws, imperfections and past mistakes, you were created purely for His enjoyment!"
–S. Kristi Douglas

A Princess Ponders...

1. How do you feel knowing that you are a work in progress?

2. Does it frustrate you? Or does it relieve you? Why?

3. Read Philippians 1:6. Who is responsible for initiating change in your life?

4. Is it possible to influence the speed of your progress in a particular area of your life? Why or why not?

5. Do you ever compare yourself to others? In what ways do you most frequently compare yourself?

6. How does comparison make you feel?

7. Do you think comparison can ever serve a positive purpose? Why or why not?

8. In what ways do you "look" like God?

9. Ephesians 2:10 calls you a "masterpiece." What are some characteristics of a masterpiece?

10. How does knowing you are a masterpiece make you feel? How does it influence the way you see yourself?

Self-Esteem Check

1. Imagine that the following gauge represents your current level of self-esteem. Mark your current level of self-esteem and today's date on the gauge.

2. Why did you place yourself there?

3. What needs to happen in order to move the needle closer to full?

Lyrical Love Letter

Listen to **"In His Eyes."** This song was written from the perspective of a self-described "daddy's girl" as she reflects on the loving relationship she had with her father. Regardless of whether or not you had this kind of relationship with your father, God wants you to experience it with Him. Do you feel cherished by God?

Journal your thoughts after listening.

APPENDIX: STUDY GUIDE

Chapter Four
The Preparation of a Princess

"Being confident of this, that he who began a good work in you will carry it on to completion until the day of Christ Jesus."
—Philippians 1:6, NIV

"Princess, you too, have been born with a wealth of spiritual assets that can and should be enhanced in ways that please the King. When you begin to cultivate these assets, God will place you in positions of influence and will give you the wisdom and courage to carry out your unique purposes as a princess in your respective royal realm."
—S. Kristi Douglas

"There are many areas of our lives which are in need of spiritual reconstruction and enhancement. It is crucial that we become aware of our spiritual flaws so that God can develop us and use us to our highest potential in Him."
—S. Kristi Douglas

A Princess Ponders...

1. Chapter 4 listed several areas which we need to develop in preparation for becoming the princesses which the King has

called us to be. For each of the areas listed below, explain ways in which you need to be developed.

◆ Eyes —

◆ Mouth —

◆ Nose —

◆ Heart —

◆ Weight —

◆ Waiting (on God) —

◆ What other area(s) has God identified?

2. Like Esther, God sometimes calls us on special "missions" that only we can accomplish. Using your unique geographic location, race, sex, age, circle of influence, etc., what is God compelling you to do?

3. Who has God given you a burden to serve?

4. How is God encouraging you to meet a specific need?

5. What resources do you need in order to accomplish this mission? *Note: it doesn't have to be an official church ministry, or a full-time job. It could be some small act of service. No matter the scale, it is all important to God.*

Begin to pray for revelation, provision, courage, timing and favor to complete the great work God has called you to do.

Self-Esteem Check

1. Imagine that the following gauge represents your current level of self-esteem. Mark your current level of self-esteem and today's date on the gauge.

2. Why did you place yourself there?

3. What needs to happen in order to move the needle closer to full?

Journal your thoughts about what you've read in the chapter and in the exercises.

Appendix: Study Guide

Chapter Five
The Purification of a Princess

"Or do you not know that your body is the temple of the Holy Spirit who is in you, whom you have from God, and you are not your own? For you were bought at a price; therefore glorify God in your body and in your spirit, which are God's."
—1 Corinthians 6:19-20, NKJV

"Whenever God anoints His daughters for a special purpose, we must also go through the process of purification or "sanctification" as it is called in the bible. Sanctification is the process of making or becoming holy, set apart, or consecrated. It is the process of advancing in holiness; where we are progressively transformed by the Lord into His likeness."
—S. Kristi Douglas

"Welcoming God means we willingly acknowledge that we belong to Him and that all we have is His. Preparing Him room means that we search our hearts, confessing our sins and courageously addressing any attitude or action that we know would displease Him. When we open our hearts to the leading of the Holy Spirit, allowing Him to live the life of Christ through us, He makes us into a beautiful dwelling place—a palace—fit for our King."
—S. Kristi Douglas

A Princess Ponders...

1. Chapter 5 listed several ways through which God purifies His daughters to make us fit for greater service to Him. What are some of the ways God has most often used in your life? Give examples of each.

   ◆ Forgiveness —

   ◆ Obedience —

   ◆ Scripture Memorization —

   ◆ Tests and Trials —

   ◆ Hedge of Protection —

   ◆ Pruning —

2. In what ways have you ever closed off God's access to your heart?

3. What areas do you believe God is challenging you to open up to Him?

4. What will you need to do in order to "prepare Him room" and to allow Him full control of your life?

Self-Esteem Check

1. Imagine that the following gauge represents your current level of self-esteem. Mark your current level of self-esteem and today's date on the gauge.

2. Why did you place yourself there?

3. What needs to happen in order to move the needle closer to full?

Lyrical Love Letter

Listen to *"Forgive Me."* This song was written from the perspective of a woman who believed her sin was so great that it might be impossible for God to forgive her. Have you ever felt this way? The Bible teaches that the only unforgivable sin is rejection of Christ as Lord and Savior. Everything else is covered under the blood of Jesus Christ. If you confess your sin to God and are willing to turn away from it, God can and will forgive you (read 1 John 1:9).

Journal your thoughts after listening.

Chapter Six

The Promises of a Princess

"For no matter how many promises God has made, they are 'Yes' in Christ. And so through him the 'Amen' is spoken by us to the glory of God."
−2 Corinthians 1:20, NIV)

"The enemy, whom the Bible calls the 'Beast' can lull us into taking a spiritual 'vacation.' He will go to any limit to destroy your testimony and your life so that you cannot be a blessing to the world. The Beast's goal is to lure you in and to hold you hostage spiritually. He wants you to become so acclimated to his (sub) standard of living that you get spiritual 'amnesia,' forgetting who you are and where you came from."
−S. Kristi Douglas

"The King will go to any limit to get you back. He purchased you and made His. You belong to Him forever, and He will not allow you to live in filth, perversion, spiritual poverty, guilt, and fear. You were designed to be holy, sanctified, righteous, and wealthy, with a clear conscience in a life of freedom and faith!"
−S. Kristi Douglas

Appendix: Study Guide

A Princess Ponders...

1. Below is a list of some typical lies the enemy tells us. Below each lie, recall a time you fell for it. How did you respond? How did God remind you of His truth in that situation?

    💎 "Follow me, and I can fulfill your desires quickly."

    💎 "Follow me and I will give you happiness, success, and prosperity apart from God and His principles."

    💎 "Follow me and you can have your cake and eat it too."

    💎 "God doesn't care about you."

💎 "You have sinned too much to live for Christ."

💎 "No one understands what you are going through."

Self-Esteem Check

1. Imagine that the following gauge represents your current level of self-esteem. Mark your current level of self-esteem and today's date on the gauge.

2. Why did you place yourself there?

3. What needs to happen in order to move the needle closer to full?

Lyrical Love Letter

Listen to ***"Daughter of the King."*** This song was written from the point of view of a woman who is awakening to the truth of what God thinks and feels about her. Regardless of what's happened in the past, God sees your future as one filled with great promise. God's great love for you is unconditional. It has nothing to do with anything you may have done or failed to do.

Journal your thoughts as you listen.

Chapter Seven
The Power of a Princess

"The weapons we fight with are not the weapons of the world. On the contrary, they have divine power to demolish strongholds."
–2 Corinthians 10:4, NIV

"Let's face it. War is not pretty. Warriors must be brave, strong, and believe with all their hearts that the cause for which they are fighting is worth risking their very lives. Although it is unpleasant and even frightening, God requires that His daughters know how to do battle with the enemy."
– S. Kristi Douglas

"We fight against a much more fearsome opponent who is alert, heavily armed and ready for battle. If we are not careful, we can easily forget about the severity of this battle. But make no mistake - our spiritual lives and future in God's kingdom are on the line. If we lose this war, we lose everything."
– S. Kristi Douglas

A Princess Ponders...

1. Identify the Enemy: The Bible says that *"we are not ignorant*

APPENDIX: STUDY GUIDE

of Satan's devices" (2 Corinthians 2:11b). This means that we can develop a sense of discernment about when and how he might attack. Although the devil has many ways of attacking us, he generally uses tried and true methods which have proven successful against us in the past. Read 1 Corinthians 10:13. What are some of the ways in which the devil tempts you to do wrong?

2. Prevent the Enemy from Advancing: It has been said that "sin teaches us more than we wanted to know, takes us further than we planned to go, costs us more than we wanted to pay and keeps us longer than we wanted to stay." When it comes to dealing with sin in our lives, we need to take an aggressive approach. We cannot just passively live with it because it will eventually choke out our growth. What are some sins God is challenging you to deal with head on? What is he asking you to do? Ask God for the courage to obey Him without compromise, immediately, so that you can advance to the next level in your walk with Christ.

3. Use Weapons of Mass Destruction: List some practical ways in which you can skillfully use each of the weapons.

   💎 Belt of Truth —

♦ Breastplate of Righteousness —

♦ Feet Fitted with the Readiness that Comes from the Gospel of Peace —

♦ Shield of Faith —

♦ Helmet of Salvation —

♦ Sword of the Spirit —

♦ Prayer —

Appendix: Study Guide

Self-Esteem Check

1. Imagine that the following gauge represents your current level of self-esteem. Mark your current level of self-esteem and today's date on the gauge.

2. Why did you place yourself there?

3. What needs to happen in order to move the needle closer to full?

Lyrical Love Letter

Listen to **"This Battle."** This song is about the internal and external battles we face as daughters of the King. Spiritual battles should be expected. But we should also expect to eventually *win* them.

Read the passionate words of the apostle Paul in Romans 7:17-20 (MSG):

"But I need something more! For if I know the law but still can't keep it, and if the power of sin within me keeps sabotaging my best intentions, I obviously need help! I realize that I don't have what it takes. I can will it, but I can't do it. I decide to do good, but I don't really do it; I decide not to do bad, but then I do it anyway. My decisions, such as they are, don't result in actions. Something has gone wrong deep within me and gets the better of me every time. It happens so regularly that it's predictable. The moment I decide to do good, sin is there to trip me up. I truly delight in God's commands, but it's pretty obvious that not all of me joins in that delight. Parts of me covertly rebel, and just when I least expect it, they take charge. I've tried everything and nothing helps. I'm at the end of my rope. Is there no one who can do anything for me? Isn't that the real question? The answer, thank God, is that Jesus Christ can and does. He acted to set things right in this life of contradictions where I want to serve God with all my heart and mind, but am pulled by the influence of sin to do something totally different."

Journal your thoughts as you listen.

APPENDIX: STUDY GUIDE

Chapter Eight
The Prayers of a Princess

"Whatever you ask in my name, this I will do, that the Father
may be glorified in the Son.
If you ask me anything in my name, I will do it."
—John 14:13-14, NASB)

"Prayer is simply having a conversation with God. Prayer involves talking and listening. We speak to God and in turn, He speaks to us. Like any relationship, this two-way exchange allows us to get to know God intimately and is the means through which we engage Him on our behalf regarding our needs, desires, and feelings."
– S. Kristi Douglas

"Prayer has the power to overcome enemies, conquer death, bring about healing, and defeat demons. God, through prayer, opens eyes, changes hearts, heals wounds, and grants wisdom (see James 1:5). The power of prayer should never be underestimated because it draws on the glory and might of the infinitely powerful God of the universe!"
– S. Kristi Douglas

A Princess Ponders...

1. Our prayers must have the following characteristics in order to be effective. Think of a time when you received an answer to a specific prayer. Write down the ways in which your prayers demonstrate these characteristics.

   ◆ Persistent —

   ◆ Purposeful —

   ◆ Persuasive —

   ◆ Powerful —

APPENDIX: STUDY GUIDE

Self-Esteem Check

1. Imagine that the following gauge represents your current level of self-esteem. Mark your current level of self-esteem and today's date on the gauge.

2. Why did you place yourself there?

3. What needs to happen in order to move the needle closer to full?

Lyrical Love Letter

Listen to *"My Soul's Praise."* This song is an intimate prayer of adoration and thanksgiving to God, simply because of who He is. Purposefully incorporate a time of praise each day, where you ask God for nothing. You only tell Him how good He is and what He means to you.

Journal your thoughts as you listen.

APPENDIX: STUDY GUIDE

Chapter Nine
The Praises of a Princess

"I will bless the LORD at all times; His praise shall continually be in my mouth."
—Psalm 34:1, KJV)

"If prayer is a conversation, then praise is a monologue."
—S. Kristi Douglas

"Praise is not optional in the life of a true daughter of the King. It is mandatory. This is because praise has a tremendous impact on activities of the spirit realm, where God operates on our behalf."
—S. Kristi Douglas

A Princess Ponders...

1. What are some of the benefits of praise?

2. Which of these benefits have you experienced? Describe your experience.

3. Which of these benefits do you still need to experience?

4. Read 2 Chronicles chapters 6 and 7. What was God's response to the praises of His people?

Self-Esteem Check

1. Imagine that the following gauge represents your current level of self-esteem. Mark your current level of self-esteem and today's date on the gauge.

2. Why did you place yourself there?

3. What needs to happen in order to move the needle closer to full?

Lyrical Love Letter

Listen to **"Highest Praise."** This is a song of invitation for the people of God to worship Him, reminding God of the awesome things He's done.

Journal your thoughts as you listen.

Chapter Ten
The Passions of a Princess

"Blessed are those who hunger and thirst for righteousness,
for they will be filled."
–Matthew 5:6 NIV

"We will never be satisfied with anything other than a true relationship with Jesus. He is the only one who can satisfy our souls. He is the Living Water. When we continuously draw from the deep well of the word of God, saturating ourselves in prayer and meditation, we will find that a relationship with Christ quenches our deepest desires and relieves our thirst for more. We will wonder why we ever sought out anything else."
– S. Kristi Douglas

"When we are introduced to God in the flesh—the One who at once gives life, yet is Life; created water and yet is Water personified—we are confronted with our own dire emptiness and thirst."
– S. Kristi Douglas

A Princess Ponders...

Many people ridiculed the woman at the well for her lifestyle.

APPENDIX: STUDY GUIDE

Even today, when divorce is common, some might criticize her for having been married five times. However, a woman in her day needed to married in order to have her needs met. She could not independently provide for herself. This woman had legitimate financial, physical, relational and emotional needs which she believed could not be met in any other way.

1. What are some of the "husbands and lovers" you've tried in order to fill a void in your life?

    ♦ Sex _____

    ♦ Drugs/Alcohol _____

    ♦ Shopping _____

    ♦ Working Out _____

    ♦ Travel _____

    ♦ Work _____

    ♦ Education _____

    ♦ Plastic Surgery _____

    ♦ Food _____

- ♦ Binging and Purging _____

- ♦ Dieting _____

- ♦ Friendships _____

- ♦ Romantic Relationships _____

- ♦ Adultery _____

- ♦ Marriage _____

- ♦ Children _____

- ♦ Social Media _____

- ♦ Fantasy _____

- ♦ Pornography / "Mommy Porn" _____

- ♦ Religion _____

- ♦ Money _____

- ♦ Gossip _____

Appendix: Study Guide

♦ Control _____

♦ Sports _____

♦ Social Status _____

♦ Pampering / Spa / Massage _____

♦ Pets _____

♦ Sleep _____

♦ Reading _____

♦ Writing _____

♦ Video Games _____

♦ Hobbies _____

♦ Meditation _____

♦ Music & Entertainment _____

List your own:

In moderation, many of the items on the list are not inherently harmful or sinful. But when we over use, misuse and rely on them to fill the void that only a relationship with Christ can fill, they become our "husbands and lovers." Used in excess, they become addictions and idols. And they will always leave us dissatisfied.

When you are tempted to use something other than God to fill the emotional void you may experience:

1. *Remember* it can't fill you up (Jeremiah 2:13).
2. *Return* to the true source of fulfillment (John 4:10).
3. *Receive* God's gift of living water through a relationship with Jesus Christ, our continuous source of contentment (John 4:13-14).

Self-Esteem Check

1. Imagine that the following gauge represents your current level of self-esteem. Mark your current level of self-esteem and today's date on the gauge.

2. Why did you place yourself there?

3. What needs to happen in order to move the needle closer to full?

Lyrical Love Letter

Listen to *"Satisfy My Soul."* This song reiterates our dependence on God for everything we need. Only God can meet every physical, spiritual, emotional void we could ever experience. Read Psalm 139. God made us and knows us intimately. We can call on Him to meet our deepest needs.

Journal your thoughts as you listen.

Chapter Eleven
The Possibilities of a Princess

"For I know the plans I have for you," declares the LORD, "plans to prosper you and not to harm you, plans to give you hope and a future."
—Jeremiah 29:11

"We must continually remind ourselves of what God said He would do for us. The enemy wants to convince us that we are forgotten. However, God is simply waiting for us to acknowledge His word of promise to us."
—S. Kristi Douglas

"When we consider our desires and the possibilities before us, there are some questions we must ask ourselves. When we honestly answer these questions, we will discover the will of God. We must be willing to act in obedience, by faith, once we understand what God wants for our lives. We should desire to say, as Jesus said, 'I have brought you glory on earth by finishing the work you gave me to do.'"
—S. Kristi Douglas

Appendix: Study Guide

A Princess Ponders...

1. Why is understanding God's will for our lives so important?

2. Read the following scriptures. What do you discover about God's will?

    ♦ 2 Peter 3:9 —

    ♦ 1 Thessalonians 4:3 —

    ♦ Psalm 37:4-5 —

    ♦ 1 Thessalonians 5:18 —

    ♦ Psalm 32:8 —

◈ Psalm 119:11 —

◈ Isaiah 30:21 —

◈ 1 Timothy 2:3-4 —

◈ Hebrews 13:20-21 —

◈ James 1:5 —

◈ 1 Peter 2:15 —

◈ Matthew 6:10 —

Appendix: Study Guide

💎 Micah 6:8 —

💎 Hebrews 10:36

Self-Esteem Check

1. Imagine that the following gauge represents your current level of self-esteem. Mark your current level of self-esteem and today's date on the gauge.

2. Why did you place yourself there?

3. What needs to happen in order to move the needle closer to full?

Lyrical Love Letter

Listen to **"I Can Do All Things."** There are times in our lives where we can't see where God is taking us. We don't know how things will turn out. We're unsure if we will be able to survive difficult times. We want to know if our dreams really will come true. This is the life of faith.

Philippians 4:13 tells us *"I can do all things through Christ who strengthens me."* No matter what lies before us, God is already there. He has already assured us that things will work out in our favor in the end.

What *"impossible"* thing are you trusting God to do?

Journal your thoughts as you listen.

About the Author

"O Lord God...let it be known today that I am your servant and have done all things at your command. ...So that these people will know that you, O Lord, are God, and that you are turning their hearts back again." (1 Kings 18:36-38)

S. KRISTI DOUGLAS

The call on S. Kristi Douglas' life is to help establish women in the Word of God. She is a lay minister of the gospel and is a singer, songwriter, playwright, and bible teacher.

She began serving in campus ministry while studying at Temple University, where she helped organize dormitory evangelism outreach. She also developed, coordinated, and taught bible studies to students.

After receiving her degree, the Lord enlarged her vision, directing her to use her gifts of administration, teaching and her talents of event-planning. In 2005, she founded Seasons Events, an event-planning ministry which designed events specifically for women of faith.

In 2009, she wrote and recorded her first single, *Daughter of the King*. The enthusiastic response to the song led her to write and produce a 15-song stageplay, *Daughter of the King: The Musical*, which debuted in 2012 and continues to run.

In 2013, she began teaching women's bible study at a local

homeless women's shelter, which led her to publish *Portrait of a Princess: The Truth About You from the King's Point of View*. The book—developed as a result of the interaction and feedback she received from the women she was privileged to serve—is now being used as a resource for women in crisis and in transition by partnering ministries who also serve these women. In 2015, she founded She Reigns Ministries, a nonprofit whose vision is "a world where every woman knows her worth."

Kristi's teaching tackles such issues as the royalty of the believer, positive self-image, and encouragement to godliness. Her teaching focuses on prayer, the character of God, and the Person of Jesus Christ.

Her music is passionate, always aiming to touch the heart of her listeners through beautiful arrangements and her thought-provoking lyrics. Her gift of story-telling shines through in every aspect of her ministry.

Kristi studied Radio, TV and Film and graduated with honors from Trinity University in Washington, DC. She has worked professionally in broadcast and cable television, as well as in the newspaper and event-planning industries.

Her greatest blessing is to be a wife and mom of three amazing children.

Email: info@SheReigns.org
Web: www.SheReigns.org

   @SKristiDouglas

   @SheReignsNC

   @TrueDOK

Who We Are
She Reigns Ministries exists to serve women who are in crisis or in transition, helping them to move beyond the barriers of their past or present challenges by offering them a God-centered view and value of themselves. This God-centered perspective enables them to become spiritually, mentally and emotionally whole women, capable of making good decisions which will positively impact and transform their lives both now and in the future.

Our Mission
To empower women in crisis and in transition to highly value and love themselves as God does, enabling them to live purposeful, productive lives.

Our Vision
A world where every woman knows her worth.

What We Do
She Reigns Ministries provides faith-based instructional and creative arts experiences designed for women in crisis, in transition and who simply sense a need for spiritual and personal transformation. We offer workshops, retreats, conferences and original creative arts programming which shares the message of God's great value and love for women and encourages them to view themselves as God does—worthy of His best—Daughters of the King of Kings.

www.SheReigns.org

PORTRAIT OF A PRINCESS (POP) WORKSHOP

Gather your girlfriends, moms and sisters for a **POP (Portrait of a Princess)** Workshop with host, author, and She Reigns Ministries' Founder, S. Kristi Douglas. Kristi shares with passion from the "priceless pearls" of wisdom in her new book, *Portrait of a Princess: The Truth about you from the King's Point of View*. During this one-day intensive seminar, you'll enjoy uplifting praise & worship and experience transformative teaching that will motivate you to begin to discover your true worth as a Daughter of the King of Kings. Women of all ages will discover the Purpose, Preparation, Power, Prayers, Possibilities of a Princess and so much more!

Email **info@SheReigns.org** or visit **www.SheReigns.org** for info.

King's Daughter Publishing

Excellence in Fine Print.

High Quality Book Design & Publishing

As an independent publisher, King's Daughter Publishing specializes in working one-on-one with new and established authors. We will walk you through the process—from manuscript to design to the finished product. Integrity is important to us. There are never any hidden fees and no lengthy contracts. You maintain all publishing rights to your work. Our desire is simply to help ensure a superior end product.

Affordable Logos & Branding

We also specialize in logo design, business cards, bookmarks, posters, email templates, postcards, and nearly any other graphic design. We understand the challenges of being a small business because we are one. We will always try to work within your budget to provide the services you need.

Our brand promise says it all...*Excellence in Fine Print.*
Let us help you get started today!

www.KingsDaughterPublishing.com

www.ingramcontent.com/pod-product-compliance
Lightning Source LLC
Chambersburg PA
CBHW050309010526
44107CB00055B/2164